"The Recess Effect brought back deep memories and great lessons. Never did I choose the teams on the school playground, yet quite often made the team, but sometimes did not (and that was painful). This thought-provoking book is simply excellent."

David Lawrence Jr., *Chair, The Children's Movement of Florida; Retired Publisher, The Miami Herald*

"The Recess Effect is a must read whether you are an aspiring leader, already in a leadership role, or trying to understand or navigate other leaders. This book cleverly breaks down human traits and dynamics that are oftentimes born on the playground and pulls those threads through to explain how they show up in the workplace and relationships in general. Highly recommended for anyone interested in being an effective leader and should be an essential element of any leadership curriculum."

Michelle Johnson-Barnes, *Ed.D., Senior Vice President for Academic Affairs and Provost, St. Thomas University*

"In my many decades of training, teaching and practicing leadership I can say that this book is a wealth of information and models to follow. This book is useful for parents, educators and results-oriented leaders. Every page has useful information and practical guidance. Every leader should make this a must read, beginning with The Recess Effect."

Bob Preziosi, *DPA, Professional Speaker, Author of The Leadership Road, Educator, Consultant, and Former Fortune 50 VP*

"Leaders who value opportunity and belong in teams would find this book insightful. The Recess Effect exposes how deeply our earliest social experiences shape the way we organize teams, distribute opportunity, and define belonging. Rice, Rice, and Alexakis give us both the language and the responsibility to interrupt those patterns and build institutions that enable all to thrive."

Nicole Bien, *Ph.D., Chief Community Partnership & Development Officer, International Baccalaureate Organization*

"The Recess Effect expertly navigates the complex dynamics of early childhood experiences and their influence on adult leadership roles. The authors offer a fresh perspective on why we assume certain management orientations in adulthood that stem from early psychological imprints. Bravo."

Michael Adamse, *Ph.D., Clinical Psychologist and Best-Selling Author*

"That queasy-gut feeling as we wait to get picked for a schoolyard team isn't just a memory. It is society's default leadership operating system. Rice, Rice, and Alexakis masterfully unpack The Recess Effect, which rewards charisma, dominance, and conformity at the expense of fairness, accountability, and contribution. They offer educators, managers, and executives The Apple Effect, a practical system to move beyond fourth-grade instincts and judgment and make decisions that draw the best out of everyone, including former benchwarmers still often left, decades later, watching from the sidelines."

David Rider, *Senior Political Reporter and Former City Hall Bureau Chief, Toronto Star*

"The Recess Effect offers a powerful reminder that leadership patterns rarely begin in the boardroom. By connecting childhood social dynamics with workplace behavior, the authors invite leaders to develop deeper self-awareness and design more intentional, high-performing teams."

Heather Christie, *JD, CSP, Executive Leadership Coach and President, Evolve Global*

"I have long understood the importance of "play" in our lives, but I have never considered the impact of early childhood recess experiences on the way we lead and engage as adults, until now. The Recess Effect is a valuable resource for those who want to better understand leadership or become more impactful leaders themselves."

Marisa Kelly, *Ph.D., President, Suffolk University*

How Playground Dynamics Shape Leadership

Examining how social dynamics learned in childhood play reappear in adult teams, leadership cultures, and workplace politics, this book offers a fresh lens on how organizations function and how leaders are formed.

Drawing on research in leadership, motivation, and group behavior and also decades of experience in higher education and organizational consulting, the authors introduce the "Recess Effect" to explain how early roles on the childhood playground, such as the "Pickers," "Picked," and "Benchwarmers" continue to shape team selection, inclusion, opportunity, and leadership in adulthood. They also offer the "Apple Effect," a practical framework that prioritizes contribution, integrity, and shared responsibility over visibility and dominance. Providing clear insights and actionable guidance, the book helps readers recognize these patterns and take deliberate steps to build stronger teams and more thoughtful, human-centered cultures.

This is the ideal book for anyone committed to creating environments where people can contribute and thrive, including leaders, educators, human resources, and organizational development professionals.

Larry Rice is co-founder of Northern Compass Consulting, an executive coach, and leadership consultant. He previously served as a university president and currently serves on the boards of the Helios Education Foundation and the Children's Movement of Florida.

Claire Michèle Rice is Global Head of Opportunity and Belonging at the International Baccalaureate. She brings over 28 years of experience in higher education, conflict management, organizational transformation, and leadership.

George Alexakis is a university professor, corporate trainer, and entrepreneur, spanning academia and business. He has taught, trained, and published in entrepreneurship, leadership, organizational behavior, and strategic management.

How Playground Dynamics Shape Leadership

The Recess Effect

Larry Rice, Claire Michèle Rice and
George Alexakis

Routledge
Taylor & Francis Group
NEW YORK AND LONDON

Designed cover image: Getty Images @Paper Trident

First published 2027
by Routledge
605 Third Avenue, New York, NY 10158

and by Routledge
4 Park Square, Milton Park, Abingdon, Oxon, OX14 4RN

Routledge is an imprint of the Taylor & Francis Group, an informa business

ISBN: 9781041269779 (hbk)
ISBN: 9781041269762 (pbk)
ISBN: 9781003752219 (ebk)

DOI: 10.4324/9781003752219

Typeset in Palatino
by Deanta Global Publishing Services, Chennai, India

Contents

List of Figures . . . . *viii*
Acknowledgements . . . . *ix*
Foreword . . . . *xi*
Preface . . . . *xv*

1 The Recess Effect: How Childhood Games Shape Adult Power 1

2 How Pickers Are Made 17

3 Pickers at Work: Power on the Adult Playground 28

4 The Picked and the Benchwarmers 40

5 The Apple Effect: Looking Beyond the Surface 58

6 When Leadership Perpetuates Playground Dynamics 71

7 Breaking the Cycle: From Playground to Responsibility 80

8 Outgrowing the Playground: Choosing Who You Become 96

9 Designing Cultures That Don't Recreate the Playground 108

10 Becoming the Adults We Needed 113

Index *123*

List of Figures

1.1 The Recess Effect. 9
3.1 Superstar Dynamics Model. 31
5.1 Key Leadership Expectations 62
5.2 The Apple Effect 67
7.1 Leadership Styles and Their Impact on Culture 89
8.1 Five-step Apple Effect Framework. 100
10.1 Cultural Stewards of PK–12 Learning Model 117
10.2 Infrastructure of Trust Building. 120

Acknowledgements

We are grateful to the many individuals and communities that contributed to the development of this work. This book grew from years of classroom conversations, leadership seminars, research collaborations, and difficult but necessary dialogue about belonging, power, and responsibility. We thank the educators, students, executives, and colleagues who allowed us to observe, question, and refine the ideas that became the foundation of the Recess Effect and the Apple Effect.

We are especially appreciative of the editorial team at Routledge for their guidance and stewardship throughout the publication process. Their thoughtful engagement strengthened both the clarity and structure of this manuscript. We are also grateful to the scholars and practitioners whose research and lived examples informed our thinking and challenged us to deepen our analysis.

This work reflects a shared belief that leadership is not merely positional, but relational and developmental. Many individuals modeled the kind of steady, responsible leadership this book advocates. Their influence appears throughout these pages.

Individual Reflections

Larry A. Rice

I am deeply grateful to my co-authors, Michèle and George. This book is stronger because of their intellectual rigor, honesty, and commitment. Michèle sharpened the relational heart of this work. George strengthened its theoretical foundation. Writing together was both demanding and meaningful. To our daughters, Claire and Victoria, thank you for growing up inside the questions this book asks. Watching you become thoughtful, principled adults has reinforced why this work matters. And to my mother, Beatrice, whose resilience and dignity shaped my earliest understanding of strength. Whatever balance and care I bring to leadership began with you.

Claire Michèle Rice
I would like to thank my co-authors, my husband, Larry, and George Alexakis, for their unwavering dedication to the work of building communities of belonging. Their steadfast commitment to empowering students and colleagues across workplaces and communities of practice has been a constant source of inspiration. I also want to thank our daughters, Claire and Victoria, whose insights and perspectives have deeply shaped and enriched our commitment to creating spaces where everyone can feel seen, heard, valued, respected, and included. I am profoundly grateful for the support of dear friends, colleagues, and family members whose experiences continue to inform and shape our ideas, and to the global educational communities that continue to engage in the work of belonging and leadership with courage and humility.

George Alexakis
I appreciate the family and friends who allowed us to use their personal stories. Their recess experiences added a human dimension to the manuscript. I am grateful for my wife, Joy, whose sharp mind, unstinting support, and loving kindness strengthened my work throughout this process. I am especially indebted to Larry and Michèle for their trust in my abilities and for inviting me into this important work.

Foreword

How Playground Dynamics Shape Leadership: The Recess Effect

Leadership rarely begins in a boardroom.

Long before individuals hold titles, influence institutions, or guide organizations, they are learning the foundations of leadership in far simpler spaces. For many of us, that place was the playground. What happens there does not stay there. The social patterns formed in those early environments often travel with us into adulthood, shaping how we lead, collaborate, and respond to power in our institutions.

The playground may appear to be a place of unstructured play, but beneath the surface, it is one of the earliest social ecosystems where leadership dynamics unfold. It is where children negotiate rules, build alliances, resolve conflict, and experience firsthand the impact of inclusion or exclusion. It is where young people begin to understand voice, fairness, responsibility, and belonging.

These early interactions matter more than we often realize. The premise of *How Playground Dynamics Shape Leadership: The Recess Effect* invites us to reconsider those formative experiences. The dynamics we observe during recess reveal early leadership patterns: who organizes the game, who invites others to join, who mediates disagreements, and who ensures no one is left out. The same behaviors later appear in schools, workplaces, and communities. In many ways, the playground becomes our first leadership classroom. The habits formed there, including who speaks up, who organizes, who follows, and who withdraws, do not disappear with age. They often reappear years later in staff meetings, leadership teams, and organizational cultures.

As educators and leaders, it is important to recognize that these early lessons shape how young people eventually understand their role in the world. In today's complex and rapidly evolving global landscape, the purpose of education must extend beyond academic achievement alone. Our students are growing up in an interconnected world filled with both immense opportunity and significant challenge. Through technology, they are exposed daily to global crises, social inequities, and environmental concerns in ways that previous generations were not.

It is easy for young people to feel overwhelmed by the scale of these issues; yet education holds the power to transform that feeling into something far more powerful: agency. Schools should be places where students learn not only about the world's challenges but also about their ability to influence them and work with others to address them. They should be environments where curiosity is encouraged, empathy is cultivated, and purpose is discovered. When students believe that their actions matter, even in small ways, they begin to see themselves not as bystanders, but as active contributors. Those early experiences often shape how individuals later participate in teams, organizations, and communities, and how they understand leadership and responsibility in the broader world.

These early experiences do not simply shape students while they are in school, but they also shape the adults they eventually become. The same instincts children develop on playgrounds—seeking belonging, navigating hierarchy, testing fairness, or withdrawing after exclusion—often resurface later in professional life. In boardrooms, classrooms, nonprofits, and governments, adults continue to negotiate many of the same social dynamics they first encountered during recess.

This is where the connection to the playground becomes particularly meaningful. On a playground, children learn how communities function. They learn that participation requires listening, compromise, and courage. They discover that belonging does not happen automatically; it is something that must be intentionally created. These experiences form the early foundations of leadership rooted in empathy, collaboration, and responsibility, qualities that later shape how individuals participate in teams, organizations, and communities.

The role of adults in shaping these environments is equally important. Children do not simply learn from what adults say; they learn from what adults model. The way adults listen, include others, navigate disagreement, and show respect becomes a powerful blueprint for how young people learn to lead. Role modeling, therefore, sits at the heart of both meaningful learning and responsible leadership.

When educators and organizational leaders demonstrate curiosity, kindness, humility, and a willingness to learn alongside others, they reinforce the values that nurture flourishing communities. Students observe these behaviors closely. They notice when adults treat others with dignity, when they show courage in difficult conversations, and when they act with integrity. Over time, these lived examples often become more influential than any lesson delivered through a textbook.

In the chapters that follow, the authors explore how schools and organizations can intentionally cultivate these leadership capacities. They challenge the idea that academic excellence and authentic learning must exist in opposition. The deepest learning often occurs when students engage with meaningful challenges that connect knowledge to real-world action.

When individuals are given opportunities to collaborate, serve others, and address issues that matter to them, their understanding deepens. They develop not only strong academic skills but also the critical thinking, empathy, and resilience necessary to navigate complexity.

At the heart of this work lies the concept of human flourishing. Education should not be limited to preparing students for examinations or future careers. It should also prepare them to contribute meaningfully within the organizations and communities where they will live and work. Its broader purpose is to help individuals develop meaning, well-being, and a sense of responsibility toward others. Flourishing involves intellectual growth, emotional health, strong relationships, and the desire to contribute positively to society.

Schools play a central role in cultivating these conditions. When students feel valued and included, their capacity to learn expands. When they engage in service and authentic problem-solving, they develop purpose. When they see adults modeling compassion, courage, and integrity, they begin to understand what leadership truly looks like.

The "Recess Effect" reminds us that leadership is fundamentally relational. It emerges through everyday interactions involving listening, inclusion, cooperation, and care. When leaders fail to recognize how early social patterns influence behavior, organizations can unintentionally recreate the same dynamics of exclusion, hierarchy, and silence that many people first experienced on the playground.

Ultimately, the goal of education is not simply to prepare students for the future; it is to empower them to shape it. And often, that journey begins in the simplest of places, during recess, where young people first learn what it means to belong, to follow, to lead, to flourish together, and ultimately to shape the communities and institutions they will one day inherit.

~Kam Chohan
Executive Director
The Educational Collaborative for International Schools

Preface

What does it feel like to be the last child picked for a team while on the playground? All three authors of this book understand what it means to face challenges and disparities from an early age. Even though Larry, as an African American male raised by a single mother in the South of the United States, was fast and strong enough to be chosen during team selections, often after some hesitation, he couldn't help but notice how the choices of those picking teams could profoundly affect the children left behind. Michèle, as a Haitian immigrant, wondered growing up in the US whether her peers' perceptions of her background impacted how much they were willing to include her in certain activities. George grew up in the Canadian school system as a Canadian-born descendant of Greek immigrants. Additionally, not always being the tallest among his peers until he later experienced a growth spurt in his teens, George's insights added yet another layer to our collective understanding of the Recess Effect and its impact on our adult experiences in the workplace.

It wasn't just about the game or physical activity; it was about the social and emotional bonds formed during those moments, connections that had the power to shape each child's sense of belonging and future trajectory.

This book uses a very familiar phenomenon with which most adults and children can identify, the grade school playground free time period often called recess, as an analogy to explore teambuilding dynamics in organizations. During recess periods in school, children learned to play with one another, often by selecting teams. This is also the time when playground bullying would take place, or the exclusion of children considered less desirable by their classmates would take place.

The authors propose that what began in kindergarten as a strategy for encouraging independent interaction among children actually set into motion a counterproductive practice that fostered multiple fragmented communities among children. The counter effect of the various activities and cliques that children learn in kindergarten is perpetuated throughout the progressive stages of their matriculation through school. We propose that this phenomenon may yield adults who exercise the same practices and norms within the workplace, and even in their personal lives. We believe the earlier playground dynamics in our lives shape our current ways of experiencing group dynamics and ultimately may even shape our leadership styles. We refer to this phenomenon as the Recess Effect.

Some people might ask, "But hasn't recess been removed from most schools today?" While that is true, the phenomenon of recess yet exists in the form of hybrid programs and other opportunities for social interaction. The intention of this book is not to oppose recess for children; on the contrary, it seeks to promote the original intent of recess, which was to encourage social development. The authors draw on childhood lessons at recess only to glean from them valuable insights for the kinds of obstacles to work effectiveness that employees face in their adult lives. In short, the focus on exploring childhood recess is to illustrate how a set of social constructs internalized during youth can form anti-teambuilding tendencies in children and what the far-reaching effects of those tendencies in their adult lives might become.

During recess at our schools, there were usually two children picking team members, and it always felt like the rest of us were holding our breath, waiting to see if we would make the cut. We remember the fear and anxiety some of our classmates experienced during those moments, hoping, almost desperately, not to be the one left standing alone. Though some of us were often picked early because we were athletic or considered smart, we still understood what it meant to feel different. At times, we were teased because of our backgrounds or for not quite meeting expectations because of how we looked, how we spoke, or how others viewed us, and those moments stayed with us. These experiences deepened our understanding of what it means to be left out or singled out, even when we appeared to belong.

As Larry reflected, "That's when I decided to stand up for others, friends, family, or classmates, who were overlooked or bullied. I fancied myself a 'paraclete of justice,' stepping in to support those who felt left out or targeted for reasons they couldn't control."

But what about the children who were never picked at all? How did they feel? As Larry grew older, he began to see how this pattern of being overlooked extended far beyond the playground. It crept into our education, workplaces, and careers, shaping lives in ways that mirrored those team selections from our childhood.

These observations and experiences led Larry to explore the long-term effects of what he calls the "Recess Effect" and ultimately co-write this book. The systemic practices of picking, or vying to be picked, often learned during childhood and carried into adulthood, create environments where some individuals, referred to here as 'Benchwarmers', are overlooked or underutilized. As Larry and his co-authors look back on their own life experiences, both personally and professionally, they can now see much more clearly how these playground roles play out in everyday interactions in workplaces: those who Picked, those who were Picked, and the Benchwarmers.

The first-person accounts in the first three chapters of this book stem from Larry Rice's personal experiences as a university professor and administrator. Having spent nearly 30 years examining all three roles, two profound observations and questions ring true for Larry: (1) what happens when children begin playing within one of those roles and remain functioning within that role throughout their childhood into adulthood?; and (2) what would happen if these roles were better understood by teachers, school administrators, parents, and later as adults, by workplace leaders and line managers? Thus, the goal of this book is to offer insight into the three roles: the Pickers, the Picked, and the Benchwarmers. We will examine these roles as they emerge on the playground and how they are later manifested in adult workplaces while providing readers with opportunities for self-reflection, growth, and the chance to make adjustments, both personally and professionally.

Throughout the book, we share personal stories and real-life anecdotes that illustrate how childhood moments continue to echo into adulthood. These reflections are drawn from research, university classroom exercises, conversations, and lived experiences across decades that are meant to foster a deeper connection with readers. We invite our readers to revisit their own formative experiences and consider how they may have impacted their personal growth as well as that of others.

At its core, *How Playground Dynamics Shape Leadership: The Recess Effect* is about more than just school recess time and playground antics. It highlights how our childhood experiences shape us and shows how we can use that knowledge to improve our relationships with others in our workplaces and through our social interactions and ultimately, to build a better future for ourselves.

~From the authors: Larry Rice, Ed.D., Claire Michèle Rice, Ph.D., and George Alexakis, Ed.D.

1

The Recess Effect

How Childhood Games Shape Adult Power

Commonly held views from the behavioral sciences suggest that repressed childhood memories affect adult human actions. School playground, often referred to as recess, periods that seek to facilitate social assimilation among children, often result in childhood alienation due to peer interactions. To what degree do childhood experiences affect the actions of their adult selves in the workplace? In seeking to answer the question, I began what I now refer to as the Recess Effect Experiment with my leadership courses. The following story chronicles the start of this journey.

Larry's Story: A Case in Point

I began my career as a professor and chief academic officer, later serving as a vice president and eventually as a university president. Throughout my academic career, I continued to provide strategic management, leadership development, executive coaching, conflict resolution, and teambuilding consultation to businesses across the United States and the Caribbean. Among all these roles, I found the greatest fulfillment during my years as a university professor. Teaching and learning were my elements, and this brought me joy. Today, as a leadership consultant, I find the same reward when working with clients across diverse

DOI: 10.4324/9781003752219-1

industries. Whether engaging college students or organizational teams, my approach has involved using reflective training activities to bridge the theory-practice gap, creating new insights that lead to new actions, a process often referred to as praxis (McNiff, 2013).

When I was a young professor, I was delighted to learn about my assignment to teach a new course in leadership studies. Having taught leadership in both community and university settings multiple times before, I approached the course with a flexible mindset, aiming to adapt to the unique needs of the students. That leadership course was composed largely of non-traditional students. Many were first-generation college students, while others were in the midst of career transitions. The class reflected a wide range of backgrounds, including differences in culture, socioeconomics, age, and life experience, with an equal balance of men and women. I knew from the first day that this classroom experience was going to be unique.

Teaching the course was a rewarding experience because I had the opportunity to work with one of the most dynamic and richly varied groups of students I had encountered in years. By the end of our time together, the students and I had learned invaluable lessons about what makes us leaders.

The leadership class was an 11-week course that met twice a week for 2 hours each session. The 2-hour block provided the perfect conditions for a leadership course because it gave me the opportunity to utilize myriad modalities in the classroom and to stray from the pure lecture approach. Usually, I began a session by going over the day's objectives and giving a 15–20-minute slide deck presentation on the scheduled topic. I would then divide the group into teams and use a group dynamics training method to encourage interaction.

The approach necessitated grouping participants in a team-building exercise and asking each group to identify a group facilitator, a note taker, and a reporter. Each group agreed collectively on the facilitator, and the facilitator's role was to ensure that the team worked together to accomplish whatever exercise was assigned in an inclusive manner.

After the group exercise concluded and each reporter presented, I wrapped up the discussion and introduced the next topic, which might include a case study, video assessment, or another related assignment. As the weeks went by, the group became increasingly aware of emerging management challenges and the factors that separate leaders from managers.

During the first 6 weeks, the focus was on teambuilding, motivating, coaching, communication, conflict resolution, change management, and strategic leadership. The students were not only responsive to the class sessions, but many engaged me outside of class to discuss topics that ignited positive debate during class time.

The topic that sparked the most discussion was teambuilding. In one of the lessons on teambuilding, I asked the class whether differences in identity, background, and experience posed the greatest challenge to building effective teams within a corporate setting. In other words, could the composition of a group make it harder for a supervisor to bring everyone together? Some students wanted to unpack what we meant by "identity, background, and experience," so we agreed on a working definition. For our discussion, any characteristic that sets someone apart, such as socioeconomic status, gender, religion, culture, physical ability, age, experience, or academic credentials, would count as a factor worth examining.

With this understanding, I divided the class into groups, but the students struggled to agree on how the groups should be composed. Some argue strongly that identity, background, and experience have little or no effect on teambuilding. From one of the groups' perspective, teambuilding is merely a matter of communicating effectively. Other students maintained that identity, background, and experience *did* play important roles, and that people should perceive these elements as benefits rather than as threats. Some students were quite passionate about their positions.

I had 38 minutes remaining in that day's class. I felt that this was an opportunity to boost my lessons on teambuilding and diversity. I wanted the students in my classes to understand the nature of true teambuilding. I wanted them to learn what leaders require to foster a teambuilding community in the workplace. Where better to start than to take the students back to the origin of the planted seeds: Kindergarten.

A Kindergarten Analogy

I often tell leadership students that their kindergarten teachers taught them some of the best leadership techniques. As such, I enjoy taking students back to their kindergarten years to remind them of the value-centered lessons that they learned but have likely forgotten. On that fateful day, I shared the following with the class:

> Your kindergarten teacher taught you the importance of apologizing to others when you made a mistake that hurt them. Your kindergarten teacher told you to "play nice." Robert Fulghum used the simple credo, "All I Really Need to Know I Learned in Kindergarten" to write and entitle his #1 New York Times bestseller.
>
> (Fulghum, 1988)

How many corporate executives have long forgotten the valuable lesson, "play nice!"? Better yet, how many of us have forgotten those words that, had we kept them in mind, might have assisted us in influencing others in the workplace today? I always remember my kindergarten teacher looking down at me and saying, "Now, why won't you just turn that frown upside down?" Though the words may sound silly or even simplistic to an adult, as a child, I could not help smiling.

Our teacher was giving us a valuable lesson: we should not take life so seriously, but we should instead lighten up, enjoy our day, and look on the bright side. How many of us could use these words of wisdom and encouragement from our kindergarten teacher today? If these teachers could see us now, how many of us would they observe spending more time frowning than smiling?

Another bestselling author, Jon Huntsman, argued in *Winners Never Cheat* that the values that lead to lasting success are not new. They are the same principles many of us learned as children but gradually abandoned, including the belief that "you can do well by doing right" (Huntsman, 2005). Old-fashioned values, he suggests, do not expire simply because culture evolves.

Developmental research reinforces this point. Peg Dawson and Richard Guare explain that executive skills formed in childhood shape everyday functioning, from self-regulation to planning and follow-through (Dawson & Guare, 2003). Although their work focuses primarily on children and adolescents, the implications extend further. The habits formed early do not disappear. They mature.

This observation lies at the heart of the Recess Effect. When exclusionary behaviors go unaddressed during formative years, they can harden into adult patterns that undermine inclusive community building at every level.

I decided to begin with an experiment, using the class itself as the subject. I challenged my leadership students with a simple question: What are the potential effects of individual differences on teambuilding? As I watched them wrestle with the assignment, I found myself thinking back to kindergarten, and even to my daughters' early classroom experiences. Some of the most powerful leadership lessons are introduced in those formative years, yet the unconstructive ones often linger longer than the positive ones teachers try to instill. Kindergarten, in many ways, becomes the earliest case study in leadership.

The Experiment: Part 1—The Recess Effect

As I stood before the class, looking at their attentive eyes, the students continued to argue if individual differences had a negative effect on teambuilding. I asked them to close their eyes and reflect back on their childhood. What I then shared unfolded as follows:

> *Visualize if you will, your days in kindergarten. Do you remember how much fun you had and how often you and your classmates played together? Can you recall the kid you enjoyed playing with the most? Can you visualize your teacher and remember some of the encouraging words she said to you*

> *when you were sad? Do you remember the part of the day you enjoyed most? Was it lunch time?* (With their eyes closed, some of the students nodded their heads in an affirmative response.) *Or was it that one time during the day that all children looked forward to? . . . Recess.* (Most of the students in the leadership class nodded yes.)
>
> *Recess was indeed the time during the day to which most of us looked forward. Can you recall why you enjoyed recess so much?* (Some of the responses were "fun," "games," "running," "swinging" and "jumping.") *Can anyone recall ever having a bad experience during recess in kindergarten?* (No one could.) *Can you picture the kid you played with the most?* (Heads nodded yes.) *What made that person special? What did you have in common with that kid? Can you remember?* (Heads nodded yes.) *Was it that you liked the same toys or enjoyed playing the same games? Was it because the kid was closer to your height or size? Did anyone have a favorite kindergarten pal who was of the opposite sex?* (No one did.) *Now, can you remember whether the girls played with the girls and the boys played with the boys?*

Most of the students nodded yes, but some did not nod at all, as though they were confused. I asked the class whether they could think about their sixth-grade year. Because it is easy to remember, I asked them to visualize recess during the sixth grade. Yet many would rather not remember it at all. Sixth-grade recess concludes the progressive stages of what occurs from kindergarten through fifth grade. Elementary school students make the transition from elementary school to middle school at this scholastic level. The transition from fifth grade to sixth grade should not be underestimated. What children observe and practice during recess at this level can be quite different from their previous experiences. Some of what children encounter during primary school years provides much of the basis for what *not to do* in teambuilding.

Consequently, I asked the class to remember the activities that occurred during recess from kindergarten to sixth grade and to name a few of them. Students mentioned games such as kickball, soccer, volleyball, baseball, basketball, and relay races.

In that moment, I gave a name to something most of us had experienced but never examined. I called it the Recess Effect.

The Recess Effect Defined

During recess, games would often spring up naturally across the playground. At first glance, the scene looked ideal: kids laughing, running, yelling, and jumping with carefree energy. But a closer look revealed something else entirely. You could begin to see how quickly children learned to form groups, stick with their own, and leave others out. Cliques weren't formally taught. They were absorbed, modeled, and practiced in real time in the schoolyard. Most children fall into three essential categories when playing games, sports, and other team activities: the *Pickers*, the *Picked*, or the *Benchwarmers*. Most adults will easily remember the category to which they belonged. I introduced students in my classes to each of the categories and explained the dynamics of the playground in elementary school by describing my own childhood experiences. I shared my experiences so that they could see how these roles also play out in life's playground.

As a child, I was rather short for my age, but I was very assertive, talkative, fast, and somewhat strong. I normally fell into the category of the Picked. The terms 'Pickers,' 'Picked,' and 'Benchwarmers' are used here to describe the roles children often find themselves in during the team-selection process at recess. These roles do not reflect an individual's worth or capability but instead illustrate how social dynamics naturally unfold. As adults, these early patterns of social interaction often influence how we perceive and interact with others in professional environments. As we revisit these childhood roles, it's essential to ask ourselves: How do we, as adults, perpetuate or dismantle these dynamics in our workplace? By understanding the origins of these behaviors, we can take intentional steps to foster more cohesive, inclusive, and productive team building.

The Pickers

The Pickers were the children who had an outstanding quality that positioned them in the forefront on the playing field during recess. These qualities could include any of the following characteristics: assertiveness, aggressiveness, self-confidence, courage, and enthusiasm. The Pickers often may have been bigger, older, or more charismatic children who were extroverts. The Pickers were the popular children on the field, and these socializers usually participated in the recess activities. Not only did they participate, but they could also select whom they wanted on their teams.

The Picked

The playground social order ranked the next-in-line Picked in nearly as high esteem as the Pickers. These individuals either were friends of the Pickers or were skillful at the schoolyard games played. The Picked generally felt quite content and took pride in the Pickers choosing them, depending on how frequently it occurred and which Pickers chose them. The Picked also shared many of the Pickers' qualities, but perhaps not visible enough to make them Pickers. However, it was common for the Picked to become Pickers as they acquired more skill or popularity.

The Benchwarmers

Were there children who did not play on either team during recess? The answer: yes! Who are the *Benchwarmers*? The following illustration, which depicts children playing during recess, implies that the children enjoy the various activities presented to them, at first glance. You will notice that Figure 1.1 indicates many counterproductive situations once you examine the depiction more thoroughly.

The Experiment: Part 2

After explaining the categories of children in recess to my leadership class, I walked around the room. I wondered who among them were the Pickers, the Picked, or the Benchwarmers. Curious, I tried an exercise to find out. I told the class that I wanted five volunteers for a team activity. I initially gave them no further hints about what was to come. I asked the first five who agreed to join me at the front of the class to explain that we were going to

FIGURE 1.1 The Recess Effect
Artwork by Claire Rice.

try a different approach to teambuilding. I handed them the class roster with all of their classmates listed. I asked the volunteers to serve as team leaders, and I gave them ten minutes to strategize among themselves about how they would form their teams. When the 10 minutes were up, I instructed the team leaders to list their names and those of their respective team members on the board.

I discreetly asked the team leaders to use my roster for help remembering the names of their peers and assessing who was present. While the team leaders were in a corner strategizing, I walked around the room asking some of the other students whether they were able to identify with the recess scenario that I had shared with them; everyone nodded in agreement.

As I walked up and down the aisles, I turned to several of the remaining students and asked, "So which one were you: a Picker, a Picked, or the Benchwarmer?" Some identified themselves as Pickers. Others admitted they were among the Picked. I then looked at a female student, Ms. Sally Broaden, and asked her the same question. Her response was noteworthy. She responded, "I was the Benchwarmer. As a matter of fact, I was never a Picker, and I was never among the Picked." Students who heard the comments seemed somewhat startled by Sally's response, delivered in a sad tone. Just looking into her eyes, I could see that she not only identified with the scenario, but that I had perhaps struck a negative chord and reopened an old wound.

The Benchwarmer category was the most interesting group of children during recess. The Picked often did not select certain children at all! Since teams needed an equal number of players on each side, the less desirable children were the odd ones out and frequently excluded completely. The unselected child was usually the passive one and did not make waves when left out during the picking process. In instances when the Benchwarmer child did have the opportunity to participate, it was frequently the result of a teacher's intervention.

Because of Sally's disclosure, I was actually relieved when the volunteers yelled: "We're ready, Dr Rice!" I looked over at the board and saw that the team leaders had listed their respective team members. I asked the first team leader to call out her teammates. She cheerfully and proudly announced her team members. I then went down the line, allowing all the team leaders to announce their team members. The picked students joined their team leaders and formed mini circles to prepare for a teambuilding exercise. I then presented a case study pertaining to a dysfunctional team in which the team had to analyze the problem and formulate a solution. After deliberating for 20 minutes, the team reporters presented the team's conclusions. While the case study offered an opportunity for teambuilding, the true lesson was yet to occur. I noticed the time, wrapped up the discussion on teambuilding, and dismissed the class.

As the other students were leaving, Sally approached me and asked, "Did you see what happened?" I had no idea what she meant and asked, "What are you referring to?" "I was never picked," she said. As Sally looked at me for a response, I was speechless. I am both a researcher and an empath. I had no idea how to feel, excited or devastated. My excitement would come from the knowledge that this experiment's outcome was exactly what I hypothesized. Even under controlled conditions, such as volunteer selection, whenever a process allows individuals to choose their team members, the threat of overlooking a peer always exists. Somehow, someone may go unnoticed or be the last one picked. The volunteers saw themselves as team leaders; they were, in fact, the Pickers. The Pickers selected the Picked and, consequently, Sally became the Benchwarmer. The experiment was a success. Nevertheless, the fact that they did not select Sally disturbed me. The one student who identified herself in the classroom as being among the Benchwarmers growing up was the one student not picked during the experiment. The irony was uncanny.

I asked Sally, "Meet me in my office in 10 minutes so that we can discuss this further," though I had not begun to formulate the words that I would use to console her. She agreed to meet me, and I hurried to my office to collect myself and consider what I was going to say. When Sally arrived, she tearfully sat across from my desk. I asked her how the course was going overall. Her response was that she enjoyed the class and that she was learning a lot. However, she went on to explain that the Recess Effect scenario described at the beginning of that day's class had upset her because it reminded her of how she felt when those who picked teams on the playground in elementary school overlooked her.

Those feelings had resurfaced when the exercise began, and Sally could not understand why no one had picked her, yet again. "No one wanted me on their team today," she said. I reassured her that nothing like that was going on. "This entire exercise was conducted to provide a practical demonstration that would expose the Recess Effect for what it is, a socially accepted practice that appears to be inclusive but actually fosters exclusion. It was not just for the purpose of the teambuilding exercise." I assured Sally that her classmates had no ill intent by not selecting her. "But you even gave them your class roster so that they would not miss anyone," she replied. By this time, Sally had begun to weep incessantly, but she asked me not to be concerned because she had grown accustomed to such treatment. I explained to Sally that this was the initial phase in the Recess Effect Experiment and that I would revisit that day's session in two weeks.

By that time, I would have presented and conducted training on conflict resolution, civility, and sensitivity. I assured Sally that I would offer more explanation of the experiment at that time. However, I explained, there was a process that she and her classmates had to undergo to move from the fragmented attitudes that recess team selection had reinforced since kindergarten to a more inclusive way of thinking. The two upcoming training sessions would provide a foundation to prepare the class for a more revealing discussion on the Recess Effect. I asked Sally whether she would be willing to wait and have patience until that time. "Fine," she said. "But there's not much that can change what happened." We will examine the conflict resolution training session as well as the presentation on civility and sensitivity later in this book. Meanwhile, I now offer you the results of the experiment.

The Experiment Part 2: Exposing the Recess Effect

Two weeks had passed since the class team exercise, and it was now time for a reality check. I began by asking the class to recollect the teambuilding debate that we had two weeks prior. Everyone remembered the highly engaging discussion. I asked them whether they could recall the presentation that I gave on the Recess Effect. They all remembered it. I then asked for thoughts and insights on the exercise and inquired about anyone's observations about the correlation between the presentation and the Recess Effect.

Some students said they thought the volunteer approach to choosing leaders, who would in turn choose teams, was a good way to prevent the Recess Effect from occurring. Others agreed but still felt the selection process was uncomfortable. For example, "I was just hoping that someone was going to select me early and write my name at least in the top three," said Justin. "How interesting!" I replied. "I'm sure your hope was shared by others." I was delighted to see this as further evidence that the experiment had worked. I asked the team leaders to come to the front of the class so that I could begin to illustrate the real lesson and purpose for the teambuilding exercise. I told them that team-selection methods often prevent highly effective team-building efforts because they contain flawed, counterproductive, and detrimental elements.

While the team leaders stood at the front of the class, I asked them to call their teammates to join them once again. When the first leader called her team, everyone seemed excited. Many students were smiling, cheering, and shouting: "Yeah, the 'A' team!" As the second and third team leaders called their groups, I started to observe Sally's body language. She was reserved, but I knew that she could handle this. When the last team leader called his group to the front, the laughter and facial expressions began to fade. He called the last group member in his team. What had been apparent to Sally and me for the last two weeks now dawned on the other students. Then it hit them. There were not one, but two students left unchosen. Sally and Ralph were still sitting.

The class became so silent that I could hear the student next to me breathing. His heart and mine were both racing in anticipation of another lively and volatile discussion. As the students stared at Sally and Ralph, I addressed the class:

> *Now, can you see the danger? Consider what just happened. No one selected Sally and Ralph to serve on a team! For you, it may have appeared as just another group activity, maybe even a dramatic exercise on teambuilding. However, this was more than that. This was my way of sharing with you the true nature of what I call the Recess Effect. I called you team leaders, but you were Pickers. As you selected your teams, they were the Picked. What we did not avoid in this class was what, unfortunately, occurs quite frequently when the Pickers select the Picked. There remained the Benchwarmers after the Picker made their selections.*
>
> *Sally, how does it make you feel that no one picked you? [A tentative silence occurred for about 10 seconds.] "For the past two weeks," Sally replied, "I've felt like shit. Not only was I not picked to be on a team, but as everyone started to go into their groups, the room was filled, so no one even noticed that I wasn't actually in a group." I looked over at Ralph and asked him how he felt about the Pickers not picking him. "I really didn't care*

> *about not being picked," Ralph said. "It just seemed strange that even though they had a roster, I wasn't chosen. When I realized that I was not selected, I decided to just blend in and played it off as though I was selected on a team." "I knew about Sally's situation," I confessed to the class. "However, I was unaware that Ralph was not picked. I would suggest that each of you consider the team selection process that we went through."*

The workplace often warrants or requires the selection of teams. While statistics vary and most put the percentage much higher, one can safely conclude that at least 50% of the workforce collaborates in groups identified as teams (Battistelli & Ashby, 2022; Katzenbach & Smith, 2015; Mohrman & Mohrman, 2014). The increasingly common emphasis on team processes and shared experiences may seem beneficial to those involved. But what truly drives this behavior? Is it a commitment to group-oriented values or team-first mindsets? Consider the moments when managers, whether intentionally or not, exclude certain individuals from teams. These decisions may reflect deeper assumptions about who fits into the team culture and who does not. Think through how managers select teams for projects or special assignments. What are the implications for those who aren't chosen? *The Recess Effect* illustrates how the team-selection habits children develop early on carry over into adulthood. Children who were once the Pickers on the playground, those who routinely chose teammates, often grow into adults who unconsciously replicate those same patterns of exclusion with their colleagues and subordinates. The initial goal of the classroom exercise described earlier was to introduce the concept of the Recess Effect. I hoped the students would begin to recognize how easily division and exclusion can emerge from arbitrary decisions about who gets selected to join a team, often based on vague or subjective criteria. Those doing the choosing, known as the Pickers, routinely leave others out. Just like children at recess, the students were drawing from their own social conditioning when forming groups, which shaped how they acted and made decisions. In the same way, many workplace teams are set up for failure from the outset.

After I had outlined the goal of the exercise with my leadership students, I noticed that as they looked at Sally and Ralph (their Benchwarmer peers), they appeared genuinely disturbed by the oversight. Sally's words added to their internal conflict, as one group leader felt compelled to explain to the class how she went about selecting her group. She said that she had selected five classmates whom she had not worked with in previous group activities, and she wanted the opportunity to get to know them better. Another team leader confessed to selecting peers whom he knew to be hard workers since he was not sure what the assignment would be and did not want to take any chances. No matter the team leaders' reasons for selecting members, overlooking Sally and Ralph signaled to the rest of the class that they still had important teambuilding lessons to learn.

The Aftermath: Navigating the Lessons of Exclusion

The experiment was a success in exposing the Recess Effect, but it also left some participants, Sally and Ralph in particular, feeling excluded. This presented an opportunity to demonstrate how leaders must handle sensitive moments with care. I knew the debrief process would be crucial to help the class reflect on their actions and understand the systemic nature of exclusion.

As the class gathered for the follow-up session two weeks later, I began with a reminder of the exercise's purpose. "We are not here to criticize individual choices," I explained. "This is about uncovering the unconscious patterns we've all internalized and exploring how to build more inclusive environments."

I asked the group to share their experiences, starting with the team leaders. Justin spoke first: "I thought I was being fair by choosing people I hadn't worked with before. But I didn't realize how it might feel for someone who wasn't chosen."

Sally's voice broke through the silence: "It's not just about this exercise. It brought back every time I was overlooked. That hurt doesn't go away."

Her words lingered, underscoring why these conversations matter. I asked the group to consider how similar dynamics unfold in real workplace settings and what it takes to build teams that include rather than exclude. Together, we began naming practical shifts: assigning teams randomly, rotating leadership, mixing skill levels, and pairing people based on complementary strengths rather than familiarity. To make the lesson real, I scheduled a follow-up session so students could report how they applied these changes in their professional lives. The message was clear. Inclusion requires reflection, intention, and consistent practice.

References

Battistelli, A., & Ashby, A. (2022). Success factors of high-performing teams: A literature review. *Team Performance Management*, *28*(1/2), 36–56.

Dawson, P., & Guare, R. (2003). *Executive skills in children and adolescents: A practical guide to assessment and intervention*. Guilford Press.

Fulghum, R. (1988). *All I really need to know I learned in kindergarten: Uncommon thoughts on common things*. Ballantine Books.

Huntsman, J. M. (2005). *Winners never cheat: Everyday values we learned as children (but may have forgotten)*. Pearson Education.

Katzenbach, J. R., & Smith, D. K. (2015). *The wisdom of teams: Creating the high-performance organization* (20th anniversary ed.). HarperBusiness.

McNiff, J. (2013). *Action research: Principles and practice* (3rd ed.). Routledge.

Mohrman, S. A., & Mohrman, A. M., Jr. (2014). Designing organizations for sustainable effectiveness. *Organizational Dynamics*, *43*(4), 282–290.

2

How Pickers Are Made

The Picker

Pickers often share a common set of traits that set them apart, even at a young age. Think back to the children who always seemed to be in charge during recess, the ones choosing the teams, setting the rules, and leading the games. What gave them that influence? Was it confidence, social awareness, physical ability, or simply a willingness to step forward? And why were certain children repeatedly placed in that role while others were not? This section takes a closer look at those early leaders, the Pickers, and examines how the playground looked from their point of view. As these children move into adulthood, we explore how those same instincts and habits resurface in professional settings, shaping how they lead, relate to others, and make decisions at work.

The Qualities of the Pickers

If you were ever a Picker, think back to your days on the playground. What was it about you that improved your status on the field? Other children seemed to gravitate towards Pickers, making them the center of attention during recess. When more

DOI: 10.4324/9781003752219-2

attention went to some, others naturally received less or were ignored altogether.

If you were a Picker, did others use the following characteristics to describe you? Pickers are assertive. They exhibit highly self-motivated and charismatic characteristics. Some leadership experts would define the word leadership as having the ability to inspire confidence in those around them (Avolio et al., 2021; Bass & Riggio, 2021; Northouse, 2021; Yukl, 2018).

Pickers possess the unique skill of getting others to lobby behind them. They often show skill in doing this, even when others do not like them. Only those with a certain confidence assert themselves as the ones who choose teammates. The act requires courage and self-esteem.

Recalling my childhood, the one Picker experience that stands out in my mind occurred while I (Larry Rice) was in fourth grade. The Picker's name was Justin, but all the children called him *Steamboat*. In fact, most of us did not even realize whom the teachers were addressing when they called out his legal name. I first met Justin during recess. Steamboat was the tallest and strongest child among us. When the bell rang for all the fourth graders to go outside for recess, we ran as fast as lightning. Once on the field, those of us who played soccer or baseball gathered in a corner at the farthest end of the field, out of the teacher's eyesight. This strategic location allowed us to play rough. As we gathered at the end of the field, one of the boys who usually picked his team members said that he was going to choose who would be on his team. He asked who would lead the other team and pick against him. Steamboat, who had just enrolled in our school, walked into the center of the group and announced, "I will pick my team. Let's play rock, paper, and scissors to decide who chooses first."

I was in awe of how confident and persuasive this young boy was. No one challenged him. I thought, who did he think he was to come onto our field to be the boss of a team and then to pick his team? His level of self-confidence was unmatched, and he soon became a permanent Picker during recess. Steamboat was a trendsetter. When he wore his pencil in his hair, other children copied him by doing the same with their pencils. He walked with self-assurance and in a unique manner. Other children followed suit.

Steamboat also had a strange but impressive nickname and imposing voice. However, his most notable characteristic was his versatile athleticism. He appeared to be competent at all field activities: soccer, baseball, basketball, dodgeball, track, etc. He was not the most athletic boy on the field, but he showed capability whenever playing in a game. Steamboat was the classic Picker. He was charismatic, skillful, assertive, friendly, and extroverted. He spoke up and seemed not to question whether he would get to participate in an activity.

Natural Born Pickers

I met Steamboat's mother, brother, and sister during my fourth and fifth grade years. Tellingly, his family always compared Steamboat to his father. They said that the boy's father was an athlete and an "attention getter." They also shared that Steamboat was tall and fast, just like his father. Steamboat would often receive comments in school, such as, "You're as tall as your father." This could be a major confidence builder. Did Steamboat get his leadership personality from his father? Many leadership experts discuss the relationship between leaders and genetics.

Another boy, whom I later noticed in my sixth-grade homeroom class, had a distinctively deep voice that commanded attention on the playground. Other boys seemed intimidated by him because he was the only boy who had that level of bass in his voice. This boy's father was a firefighter who spoke in our class one day, and his father's voice was even deeper, unsurprisingly.

Many of us inherit core qualities from our parents. My mother would say that certain physical qualities that I had, like my walk and the tone of my voice, came from my father (even though I spent very little time with him while I was growing up). So clearly, unique hereditary characteristics among leaders factor in.

While many leadership qualities aren't tied to appearance, we can't ignore the role that physiology can play in shaping one's self-regard. Studies consistently show a link between leadership success and physical characteristics, particularly traits like height and perceived attractiveness. Individuals perceived as taller or conventionally attractive are more likely to attain leadership positions in both politics and the corporate world (Judge & Cable, 2004). A comparative study on the matter concluded that characteristics associated with body size and maturity alter leadership perception and may influence the selection of leadership for Congress during the US democratic elections (Hesselbein et al., 1997). Although physical traits influence how others perceive us, they can also shape our sense of self-worth and affect how effectively we connect with others.

Since some leadership theorists support the idea of natural born leaders, the notion of naturally emerging Pickers doesn't seem far-fetched. We all inherit core aptitudes, personality characteristics, and intellectual abilities that provide a foundation for how we interact with our environment and work with others. The conditions of our upbringing shape how our core features manifest and the extent of our personal and professional success. While the Recess Effect affords Pickers an opportunity to further hone their leadership skills, its processes and actions often carry long-term consequences that extend far beyond the moment and prove more harmful than beneficial.

The Drucker Foundation addresses the phenomenon of natural born leaders (Pickers), stating the following:

> *When leadership is viewed as a non-learnable set of character traits or as equivalent to an exalted position, a self-fulfilling prophecy is created that dooms societies to having only a few good leaders. It is far healthier and more productive for us to start with the assumption that it is possible for everyone to lead.*
>
> (Hesselbein et al., 1997)

Even though Steamboat inherited traits from his father that could assist him in developing strong leadership skills, he was also very much a product of his surroundings. His skills became the center of attention and eventually detracted teachers' attention away from the achievements of other children.

Young Pickers not only learn to assert themselves early on, but they also begin to master the art of positioning, adapting to the unspoken rules of survival in competitive environments. Their struggle to be inclusive and empathetic during the selection process often overshadowed their ability to choose team members effectively. Inclusive values such as sharing, caring, trusting, and respect that produce winning teams clearly go against the outcomes the Recess Effect produces (Hesselbein et al., 1997; Todorov et al., 2005; Vogt et al., 2021). The Picker's inability to see beyond the surface characteristics of the Picked and the Benchwarmers on the playground can, in some cases, foster an elitist attitude toward others. This selective mindset may persist through secondary school and into adulthood.

Looking Through the Eyes of a Picker

Those who were Pickers often remember the joy and freedom of recess when thinking back on their childhood. But being a Picker came with pressure. Holding that position meant having to defend it. Recess, for many Pickers, was a competitive arena. Some might even describe it as a form of natural selection at play. I remember frequent disputes on the playground between children who all wanted to be the ones making the decisions. Most activities had room for only two teams, which meant only two Pickers per game. But there were always more than two children who saw themselves as leaders. As a result, several games unfolded at once, each carrying its own dynamics and tension beneath the surface.

The Pickers determined who chose sides. Among the children who would be selected, there may have been a dozen. Pickers simplified the process due to the variety of games that were being played on the field at once. If there were three different activities, there would be six Pickers. Usually, the most outspoken, persuasive, or skilled Pickers made the selection decisions. Sometimes, however, they would take turns choosing among activities. It was almost as though the Pickers had established their own rules for recess.

In an interview with an engineer, I asked him to reflect on his childhood experiences. He recalled that during recess, he focused only on children whose athletic abilities he viewed as superior to his own. For him, it was truly a game. If the field were a kingdom, he pursued the throne. The only people whom he noticed were those who were between him and the power that he sought. His fellow knights (Pickers) were his friends, but they were also his adversaries, because that was the way that he played the game. He befriended other Pickers just to get to know them better. Nevertheless, he always harbored the goal of outperforming them. Does this sound familiar?

Many adults play similar games in the workplace, do they not? In his seminal treatise, *The Art of War,* Sun Tzu discussed the importance of knowing one's enemy and being aware of their plans and movements (Sun Tzu, 2011). The character Michael Corleone in The Godfather Part II famously paraphrased this strategy as, "Keep your friends close, but your enemies closer," a line that has since become ubiquitous in everyday conversation. The logic also pervades among the workplace Pickers, many of whom now enjoy supervisory roles in organizations.

Many of the individuals I interviewed while teaching leadership studies and collecting data for this book described viewing their workplaces much like the school playground at recess. The stakes prove much greater, but the game still yields the same outcomes: exclusion of those players who cannot (or choose not to) compete at the level of the Pickers, namely, the Benchwarmers. The game also includes the rivalry among those who become the Pickers' chosen few (the Picked). At the adult level, the politics of the Recess Effect have moved from the playground to the workplace. The phenomenon can't rightly be called "office politics," because the same game plays out in the trades, healthcare, education, the arts, hospitality, public service, nonprofits, and even professional sports. Yes, even in hockey, for instance, the best players do not always get the most ice time, which would otherwise hone their skills and talent.

The Social Construction of Recess

Many Pickers are outgoing, charismatic, and assertive. Traits such as height, strength, speed, and overall athleticism often distinguish between the more dominant children in this group. Highly self-confident and naturally capable, some Pickers derive their greatest motivation from the social dynamics around them, especially in contrast to those categorized as the Picked in the Recess Effect. Pickers typically ensure they have a thorough understanding of the rules of any game they play. They tend to stay informed about the sports world and can speak intelligently about boxing, basketball, baseball, and their respective players. This knowledge often impresses the Picked and Benchwarmer children, who may not be as well-versed in these topics. Beyond sports, Pickers also stay up to date with the latest trends: whether in clothing, celebrities, movies, television shows, or video games. They actively seek information on anything likely to become a popular topic of conversation, reinforcing their social standing and influence on the playground.

The Picked children try to befriend the Pickers. They laud the Pickers' attributes with fanfare. Does the following statement sound familiar?

"Jimmy, you're so fast; you're the fastest boy out here!"
Or, "Sue, I love being on your team; your team has to win!"

They call this, *sucking up to the boss,* in the workplace. Everyone enjoys praise and accolades, which the Picked children acutely understand and use to continue securing their places among the Picked. As a second step, the Picked will seek to position themselves close enough to the Pickers to increase their chances of staying among those selected. The logic seems simple. The closer that the Picked kids position themselves to the Pickers, the greater their status and power.

Those who work for a living witness this dynamic every day: the closer an employee is to the boss, physically or relationally, the more power others perceive them to have within the organization. In fact, many people recognize a direct correlation between the proximity of one's office or workspace to that of a supervisor and the influence they wield. While the behaviors of the Picked may sometimes appear to stem from insecurity, they are often effective. Leveraging a relationship with a supervisor is not inherently wrong, but doing so at the expense of colleagues is problematic. As managers, leaders, HR professionals, trainers, educators, parents, and students become more aware of the Recess Effect, the need to adopt strategies that promote genuinely positive work and classroom environments becomes increasingly urgent. Awareness is the first, and most essential, step toward meaningful change.

As previously noted, children in the Picked category often concentrate on building false or pseudo relationships with the Pickers. Efforts to ingratiate themselves with the Pickers through praise, submission, and deference begin in kindergarten and often persist throughout life in similar work relationships.

Consider how many friends you had during school who you truly believed were your real friends. Think about what happens to children who always hear about the greatness of their field play. Such confidence builders inevitably produce a more self-assured individual. This high sense of self-confidence parallels behavioral traits that could be interpreted as de-motivators for the Pickers or the Benchwarmers. Anyone other than a Picker could interpret a Picker's actions as overconfident, arrogant, untrustworthy, and uncaring. Yet we commonly view Pickers as good leaders (and good pickers). It reminds me of how millions of people make determinations on the leadership ability of a politician based on one or more speeches they make, without attention to their moral character or their actual capacity to do the work for which they are being elected.

Interestingly, Pickers tend to seek out other Pickers to lead corporations. Executive turnover at the highest levels across the corporate world has become almost dizzying. In the calculus of human resources, such turnover is enormously costly in financial terms, time investment, and its impact on organizational development. Yet, when shareholders of major companies push for increased earnings, the appointment of a new C-level executive often serves as a timeworn strategy to generate market buzz and boost stock prices. Internally, however, these leadership changes rarely result in significant progress or transformation within the organization.

Peter Senge describes critical areas of need within companies in his classic book *The Fifth Discipline.* In it, he stated that productive companies become "learning organizations where people continually expand their capacity to create the results they truly desire, where new and expansive patterns of thinking are nurtured, where collective aspiration is set free, and where people are continually learning how to learn together" (Senge, 1990). Under the right environment, the Picked and the Benchwarmers might become Pickers, but Picker children likely end up becoming adult Pickers. Children vying for power to secure their position in the field exemplify the politics of the Recess Effect. Their adult counterparts similarly seek to secure their positions within the workplace.

Over time, children who practice the art of choosing who they want on their teams could eventually begin to formulate low opinions of their peers, the Picked, and the Benchwarmers. In more extreme cases, Pickers may come to see these peers as tools for meeting their own needs, rather than as equals. As adults, this mindset may manifest in the workplace, where similar patterns of exclusion, entitlement, and hierarchical thinking can reemerge in professional interactions and decision-making.

Many supervisors, department heads, managers, and corporate executives view their direct reports as unequal. While in Virginia, I had the opportunity to meet a few academic administrators at universities during a conference that I attended. I had an interesting conversation with a faculty coordinator from a private university. She had just started her position with her employer, and she was concerned about the structure of the university's workplace culture. She was disappointed with how the school allowed staff members to get involved in decision-making. She felt appalled by the idea that a "secretary" could participate in academic departmental discussions. She considered this "inappropriate and disrespectful" protocol on the campus. "Here I have a Ph.D., and I can't even have my own parking spot," she complained. "Why are we expected to park where the students park?" Furthermore, "how come the lower-level staffers can't park in a different location, so that we [the faculty] can have the spots closest to our building?! Every other school has priority parking."

I must admit that I was astounded at her perspective. I paused for a moment before responding, "It sounds like you guys really understand people, and that students truly do come first at your school." She stared at me for a moment, averted her eyes, and then walked off. Unfortunately, I've encountered similar attitudes across many industries. Some managers perceive those they oversee not as colleagues, associates, or peers, but strictly as subordinates within a rigid hierarchical structure. Professional credentials and titles often contribute to this sense of superiority. Moreover, organizational cultures that emphasize such credentials can reinforce invisible lines of authority, lines that extend beyond formal job descriptions and shape how individuals higher in the hierarchy interact with those below them.

The dynamics we have explored are not relics of childhood. They are rehearsals. The same instincts that shaped belonging on the playground still shape decision-making in classrooms, workplaces, and boardrooms. When we fail to recognize those patterns, we repeat them. When we name them, we begin to interrupt them. The question is no longer whether the Recess Effect exists. The question is whether we are willing to confront it.

References

Avolio, B. J., Walumbwa, F. O., & Weber, T. J. (2021). Leadership: Current theories, research, and future directions. *Annual Review of Psychology, 72*, 681–703.

Bass, B. M., & Riggio, R. E. (2021). *Transformational leadership*. Routledge.

Hesselbein, F., Goldsmith, M., & Beckhard, R. (Eds). (1997). *The leader of the future*. Jossey-Bass for the Peter F. Drucker Foundation for Nonprofit Management.

Judge, T. A., & Cable, D. M. (2004). The effect of physical height on workplace success and income: Preliminary test of a theoretical model. *Journal of Applied Psychology, 89*(3), 428–441. https://doi.org/10.1037/0021–9010.89.3.428.

Northouse, P. G. (2021). *Leadership: Theory and practice*. Sage Publications.

Senge, P. M. (1990). *The fifth discipline: The art and practice of the learning organization*. Doubleday.

Sun Tzu. (2011). *The art of war: A new translation* (J. Trapp, Trans.). Amber Books.

Todorov, A., Mandisodza, A. N., Goren, A., & Hall, C. C. (2005). Inferences of competence from faces predict election outcomes. *Science, 308*(5728), 1623–1626.

Vogt, J., Murrell, A. J., & Hunsaker, S. (2021). The impact of diversity on team performance: A systematic review. *Journal of Business and Psychology, 36*(1), 1–26.

Yukl, G. A. (2018). *Leadership in organizations*. Pearson.

3

Pickers at Work

Power on the Adult Playground

Same Game, Different Arena

What happens when Pickers become adults? What happens when they enter the workplace? Most of them become adult Pickers, exhibiting a common set of actions while interacting with others. In the case of children at a specific grade level, recess takes place in a community setting that fosters sub-communities habitually sprung from exclusionary practices. Pickers become the leaders of this marginalization practice. Recall that the Picker's personality includes assertiveness, charisma, and strong communication skills. As young Pickers mature, they begin to equate their attributes and the methods that they use to maintain their Picker statuses with leadership skills.

What children exhibit when they interact with other children as a derivative of the Recess Effect remains when they become adults. The interpersonal dynamics continue throughout adulthood in settings like higher education and the workplace. Just as they learned to position themselves on the playground in primary and secondary school, Pickers seek to do the same if they attend technical school, college, or university.

DOI: 10.4324/9781003752219-3

I once had a student named Bill who complained to me about the formation and governance of student clubs and organizations on our university campus. He referenced the cliques that develop within student organizations. He argued that the clubs always form into factions. I explained that the ability to build an effective team represents an essential skill that all of our graduates should learn. He agreed but argued that most of the groups that he joined fell short of what he would describe as a team. He gave me an illustration from his own experience.

Bill said that he was very interested in joining one of the organizations known for fundraising and community service activities. Therefore, he attended the new member orientation and found himself even more intrigued. Ultimately, he joined the organization and participated in various events and fundraisers. As his involvement increased, he noticed that the executive board did not always agree among themselves. He also observed that for some events, especially the more public ones, the board would select only certain members to participate. He felt that many of the board's decisions seemed connected to popularity rather than performance. He believed that all members should enjoy the opportunity to display their skills instead of the inequality that occurred. Some of the gatherings offered students wonderful chances to network from which only some benefited.

Bill felt that many organizations generally operated more like exclusive clubs rather than organizations inclusive of all students. A relevant postscript to the popularity viewpoint involves a fellow student who pointed out to me once in high school that the Pickers on the yearbook staff had a very high number of photographs of themselves in the yearbook every year.

I couldn't disagree with Bill. His concerns carried weight and reinforced the idea that the way people form groups shapes the culture within them. But are all groups truly teams? Some appear cohesive on the surface but operate quite differently beneath it.

Professional sports offer a visible example. Consider the National Basketball Association (NBA). Many NBA teams are built around high-profile superstars who are expected to anchor performance, serve as the emotional center of the team, and represent the organization publicly. From the outside, these teams may look unified, especially when they are winning. Yet cohesion on paper does not always translate to collaboration in practice.

Coaches often present a standout athlete as "Number One," positioning that player at the center of attention among teammates, owners, media, and fans. Over time, that elevation can shape expectations and behavior. Teammates may begin to defer, envy, or resent. The game becomes a stage not just for teamwork, but for individual validation. When performance becomes personal rather than collective, unity suffers.

Research supports what many athletes already know. Elite performers sometimes struggle in leadership roles when individual success overshadows collaboration (Williams, 2018). When personal status takes priority over shared goals, cohesion weakens (Coyle, 2009). Selection politics, favoritism, and bias in athlete development further complicate the picture, influencing who plays, who progresses, and who remains sidelined (Larkin et al., 2016; Mann et al., 2019; VandeWalle, 2019).

Figure 3.1 depicts the Superstar Dynamics Model and the complex forces surrounding high-visibility leaders. Positioned at the intersection of perceived strengths, institutional expectations, and observed risks, these individuals often experience both elevated status and intensified scrutiny. Understanding this tension helps explain why some leaders thrive while others struggle under the weight of organizational expectations.

The superstar in this model mirrors the adult Picker in the Recess Effect. The Pickers select, the Picked align themselves accordingly, and the Benchwarmers remain on the sidelines. While playing time may appear merit-based, decisions shaped by relationships, reputation, or familiarity can be found not only on playgrounds and courts, but in workplaces as well.

Other sports illustrate a different model. Soccer, for example, often emphasizes collective movement and coordinated strategy over individual dominance (Wrisberg, 2011). Even when star players emerge, sustained success depends on shared discipline and collaboration. Teams built on cohesion frequently outperform those that rely on isolated brilliance (Liew et al., 2018).

The lesson extends far beyond athletics. Many executives speak of building "teams," yet their practices promote a small

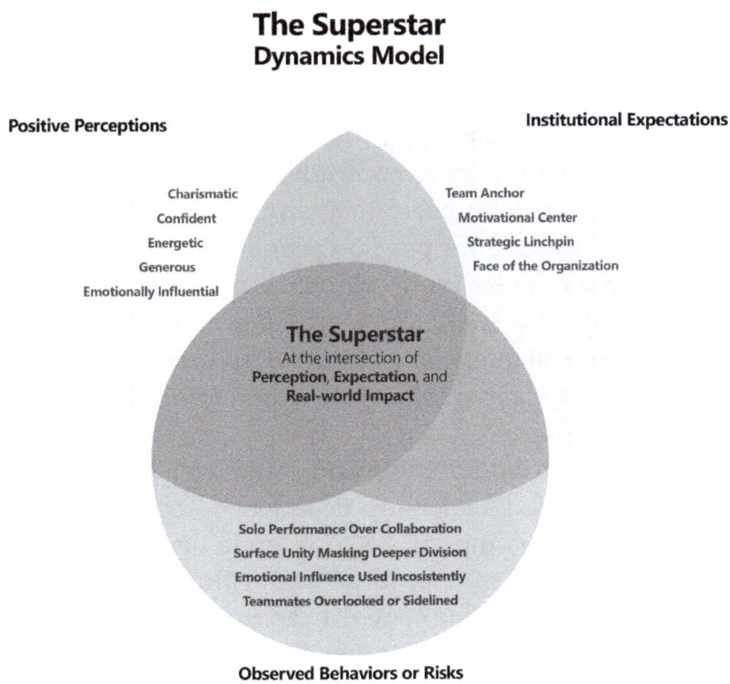

FIGURE 3.1 Superstar Dynamics Model

circle at the top while others remain peripheral. As Katzenbach and Smith (2003) observed, simply calling a group a team does not produce teamwork.

The adult Picker does not disappear after childhood. He or she matures, acquires authority, and often carries forward the same selection instincts into professional life. In this way, the Recess Effect does not fade with age. It evolves.

New Era, Old Challenges

Today's nontraditional workforce and workplace differ significantly from the norms and expectations that shaped the early 21st-century workplace, both in employee makeup and in employee expectations. The growth of the Hispanic population in the US suggests they will make up a significantly larger share of the population in the coming decades (United States Census

Bureau, 2016). Thus, the ability to understand and manage culturally diverse people will become critical. The coronavirus pandemic compelled businesses and workers to operate remotely, triggering massive changes in lifestyle behaviors and accelerating the move toward a more nontraditional workplace.

At the same time, uncertainty around Social Security and the erosion of traditional pension plans will lead more people to remain in or re-enter the workforce. Employees with physical disabilities will also make up a growing and vital segment of the labor force. The question is: *How will supervisors, shaped by the social norms and unspoken rules of the Recess Effect, successfully lead this evolving workforce?*

Jason, a good friend of mine and a manager at an advertising firm, recently shared leadership experience from his workplace. An executive at his company asked Jason to have a group of four employees develop a new product line within three weeks. The assignment was seen as a potentially career-defining opportunity.

Jason appointed a staff member, Jessica, to lead the team and allowed her to choose the other three members. She selected a graphic designer and two senior staff members who had been with the firm for more than 20 years. The team completed the project ahead of schedule and impressed the agency executive with the quality of their work.

But the success came at a cost. Two high-performing staff members resigned soon afterward. One of them was Sara, whose resignation had not yet been finalized when I spoke with Jessica. They felt overlooked and believed Jessica had selected team members she could easily outshine, those less likely to challenge her ideas or authority. One of the senior team members refused to accept any recognition and insisted, "It was all Jessica," and "Jessica should get all the credit."

Jessica was pleased with the outcome and remained unbothered by the resignations. In her view, she had simply seized an opportunity to advance her career and deliver results.

I was curious whether Jessica's actions reflected a one-time decision or a consistent pattern in her interpersonal relationships. When I had the opportunity to speak with her shortly after the project's completion, we had the following exchange:

LRice: So, Jessica, I understand that congratulations are in order for a major project the team you were on just completed.
Jessica: Thanks, I'm quite proud of my team.
LRice: Were you always this assertive and highly self-motivated?
Jessica: Absolutely. For as long as I can remember, I was always outgoing and hard working. I guess you can say I was born to lead.
LRice: When you were in elementary school, did you play outside during recess?
Jessica: Oh yes, and it was the best time for me!
LRice: Did you participate in most of the activities?
Jessica: Always, unless I was sick.
LRice: I've found that there are three prominent roles that tend to emerge during recess: those children who pick team members (the Pickers), those who are picked to play in activities (the Picked), and those who are usually not chosen (the Benchwarmers). Can you remember a similar occurrence when you were young?
Jessica: Yes! Yes! Yes! And I was always a Picker! I remember how I would be able to pick teams all the time, and I loved it! Those were great times. Come to think of it, recess was my favorite time during the day as a child.
LRice: Is it safe to assume that it has been this way for you throughout your life?
Jessica: How so? . . . you mean picking teams?
LRice: In retrospect, were your childhood experiences on the playground any different from what you experienced on high school teams or college study groups?
Jessica: I guess I was always a leader. Like I told you before, I was a born leader. I always figured out a way to drive groups. Even when I was placed in a situation where someone else was asked to be the team captain, I was still a leader.
LRice: And what qualities do you feel make you a leader?

Jessica: I never quit. I'm assertive, outspoken, and a quick thinker, and even if I'm not the smartest, I come across as the smartest because I'm very confident in myself.

LRice: When you were young, how did the other children feel about you being a picker all the time?

Jessica: I remember having many friends, and I would pick them to be on my team, of course. I think I was well-liked and somewhat popular.

LRice: Even with the children, you did not pick?

Jessica: I don't know [she shrugged her shoulders with some puzzlement].

LRice: Did you ever notice that some children were being chosen all the time and that some were being left out?

Jessica: Of course, but isn't that life? Even today, not everyone can have the same opportunities. Those who try the hardest often get what they work hard toward…don't you agree?

LRice: Actually, I spend a lot of time these days training adults who were those children who were never picked. I have a training program that teaches them how to get beyond those childhood challenges and break those vices that have caused them to be internally conflicted. Every day, we see what happens to those overlooked on the playground as children. The pattern ordinarily continues well into adulthood. They become outsiders who often find negative means to express themselves. Some adults very much fear working in teams. They can only be productive when working independently or in isolation. How did you pick your project team members on the job four weeks ago?

Jessica: I picked the three people whom I knew would get the job done and would follow me.

Author: How did your other colleagues feel about not being selected?

Jessica: Well, I realize that people are talking about quitting, but I thought they were just jealous. I really don't know what they think.

> *Author:* If you could do it all over again, would you pick the same team?
>
> *Jessica:* Well, considering what happened with people resigning and talking trash about me, I would probably ask for volunteers to see who would have wanted to work with me.
>
> *Author:* Jessica, you're in a position to win the support of your colleagues. They all know that you did a great job on the project, so your work ethic is not in question. While it may not have been your intention, your coworkers, just like the children on the playground, may have felt excluded. The gains that can come to us personally usually don't outweigh the losses that our peers endure. I would simply apologize to my disheartened colleagues if I were in your situation . . . that would be an unexpected display of strong character and true leadership.
>
> *Jessica:* What should I apologize for? If I made a mistake, then I made a mistake. We all do. But to go to my coworkers and apologize for something that they could have done themselves . . . they could have volunteered, but they didn't . . . just doesn't make sense to me.
>
> *Author:* Precisely. Is it appropriate to apologize for unwittingly hurting people? Consider saying, 'If I did anything to offend you, I apologize.'
>
> *Jessica:* You know, I'm going to call Sara [one of the two employees who resigned] and apologize if she quit on my account, just to prove to you that it doesn't matter. People aren't going to react positively to my apology. More than likely, they will not believe it anyway.

Within a few days of our conversation, Jessica contacted Sara, whose resignation was still pending, to discuss what had occurred on the project. Sara, shocked by the gesture, confessed that she felt as though none of her ideas mattered and that she viewed the project as her first opportunity to demonstrate her capabilities. However, Jessica had been so outspoken about taking the lead that everyone else gave in. The fact that Jessica did not select any of the people who had *volunteered* to be on the team caused most of Sara's dissatisfaction. When Jessica heard all of this, she responded, "Sara, I'm so sorry for what I did. I now understand that it was not fair." After their conversation, Sara went back to the firm and successfully worked with Jessica on a different project.

Mirror Images

At first glance, the relationships formed by a child Picker on the playground and an adult Picker in the workplace may appear collaborative. But this appearance is often misleading. While the group dynamic may seem productive, it can subtly fuel tension between those who are chosen and those who are left out. What looks like teamwork is sometimes only proximity, not true community. We can call this fractured dynamic discommunity. Discommunity is not the absence of collaboration, but the presence of a hidden hierarchy. It occurs when people work alongside one another without shared trust, equal voice, or mutual investment. Its symptoms include distrust, second-guessing, jockeying for position, resentment, and exclusion. Over time, these corrosive behaviors erode genuine connection and shared purpose.

An ideal environment, whether on the playground or in the workplace, encourages genuine relationship building through team activities that do not rely on a self-appointed Picker. While Pickers may foster some relationships, their methods often produce uneven or short-lived results. The common belief among Pickers that they are building strong, inclusive connections reflects the core paradox. In reality, trust is often mistaken for loyalty, and envy is confused with admiration. Although Pickers may believe their relationships are improving, over time, those relationships tend to erode.

Leadership Lessons from the Playground to the Conference Room

The situation at the advertising firm reflects what often happens during team selection in organizations across the country.

Studies show that exclusionary practices in group formation occur regularly, and our observations highlight a few key takeaways: how early socialization shapes adult behavior, how exclusion transcends gender and identity, and how leadership choices can either perpetuate or counteract these patterns (Bucher, 2004; Napier & Gershenfeld, 2004; Ng et al., 2021).

Exclusion isn't limited by gender. Both men and women engage in selective practices that can leave others out. Many of the behavioral differences we associate with boys and girls are shaped by societal expectations, not biology. In reality, most children—regardless of gender—respond to the environments that surround them. What matters most is recognizing that the dynamics of the Recess Effect cut across identity and impact everyone in different ways.

Managers have the power and responsibility to anticipate conflict. Jason's role positioned him to prevent the fallout that followed. While asking for volunteers was a good start, he could have widened the process by inviting others to express interest before assigning leadership. A simple question like, "Who else would like to be considered?" might have encouraged broader engagement. Using past performance to guide selection is valid, but the process also needs to be transparent and inclusive. Stephen Covey said it best: *"The basic task of leadership is to increase the standard of living and the quality of life for all stakeholders."* That includes creating a climate where everyone feels seen, valued, and part of the mission" (Covey, 1989).

Leaders must be mindful of how perceived authority influences group dynamics. Jessica didn't just volunteer; she publicly positioned herself as the team leader. By immediately accepting her self-nomination, Jason missed a second opportunity to model fairness and transparency. What may have begun as an earnest attempt at impartiality quickly turned into a closed-door selection process. In doing so, Jason risked not only alienating team members but also compromising his credibility as a leader.

The chapter that follows will chronicle the experiences of the Picked, including those Always Picked and those Occasionally Picked, and the Benchwarmers in the team selection process. While the chapters challenge the myth that leadership is innate, we also seek to lay bare how the workplace often mirrors these early exclusions, relegating some to roles far below their capabilities. We also introduce the idea that cultural transformation requires more than surface-level diversity; it requires rethinking who gets invited to play, and why, laying the groundwork for ways to interrupt the Recess Effect in later chapters.

References

Bucher, R. D. (2004). *Diversity consciousness*. Pearson/Prentice Hall.

Covey, S. R. (1989). *Principle-centered leadership*. Simon & Schuster.

Coyle, D. (2009). *The talent code: Greatness isn't born. It's grown. Here's how.* Bantam.

Katzenbach, J. R., & Smith, D. K. (2003). *The wisdom of teams: Creating the high-performance organization*. HarperBusiness.

Larkin, P., O'Connor, D., & Williams, A. M. (2016). Does grit influence sport-specific engagement and perceptual-cognitive expertise in elite youth soccer? *Journal of Applied Sport Psychology, 28*(2), 129–138. https://doi.org/10.1080/10413200.2015.1115332.

Liew, J., Cao, Q., Hughes, J. N., & Deutz, M. H. F. (2018). Academic resilience despite early academic adversity: A three-wave longitudinal study on regulation-related resiliency, interpersonal relationships, and achievement in first to third grade. *Early Education and Development, 29*(5), 762–779. https://doi.org/10.1080/10409289.2018.1429766.

Mann, D. L., van Ginneken, P. J. M. A., & Williams, A. M. (2019). Talent identification and the relative age effect. In A. M. Williams & R. C. Jackson (Eds.), *Anticipation and decision making in sport* (pp. 235–252). Routledge.

Napier, R. W., & Gershenfeld, M. K. (2004). *Groups: Theory and experience* (7th ed.). Houghton Mifflin.

Ng, E. S., Konrad, A., & Workman, K. R. (2021). Daily exclusionary practices in diverse workplaces. *Academy of Management Journal, 64*(3), 760–790. https://doi.org/10.5465/amj.2018.0552.

U.S. Census Bureau. (2016). *Income and poverty in the United States: 2016* (Report No. P60-259). https://www.census.gov/library/publications/2017/demo/p60-259.html.

VandeWalle, D. (2019). A goal orientation model of feedback-seeking behavior. In L. Argote & J. M. Levine (Eds.), *The Oxford handbook of group and organizational learning* (pp. 129–146). Oxford University Press.

Williams, A. M., & Ford, P. R. (2018). Game intelligence: Anticipation and decision making. In D. Farrow & J. Baker (Eds.), *Routine greatness: The psychology of peak performance* (pp. 105–121). Routledge.

Wrisberg, C. A. (2011). *Sport psychology: Concepts and applications* (7th ed.). McGraw-Hill.

4

The Picked and the Benchwarmers

The Picked

What kinds of children end up among the Picked?

Some of the most informative moments in my *Foundations of Leadership Studies* course came during an exercise I used across multiple semesters. At various points in the term, I asked students to reflect on their childhood group experiences: "Were you a Picker, one of the Picked, or a Benchwarmer?" I explained that a benchwarmer refers to a player who sits on the sidelines, someone who is rarely chosen to participate. In sports, it is a player who the coach does not select to play much (i.e., an alternate or substitute).

What followed was often telling. Several students proudly responded, "I was a Picker." Those who identified as the Picked responded differently. Their answers were less declarative and more qualified. Many felt the need to explain how they were chosen, whether it was because of athletic ability, popularity, friendship, or circumstance.

One student, Mary, offered an especially candid response. "Even though I wasn't a Picker, I was never concerned about

DOI: 10.4324/9781003752219-4

being picked because I always was. I was with the Picked!" I had only asked for her role, but she volunteered more information, as if to make clear that her inclusion had never been in doubt.

At that point in our discussion, we hadn't talked about how it felt to wait to be picked, or the emotional weight of that uncertainty. So, I asked her, "How did you feel about being picked?"

She replied, "I guess it was okay, because at least I knew who liked me the most. You know how, when you're a kid, girls pretend to be your friend, but during recess, you find out who your real friends are. A real friend wants you on her team."

I felt this confirmed a core part of the Recess Effect, so I probed a bit further. I asked whether she had ever been a Picker, and what she thought of those who were.

Her tone changed. "I didn't want to be a Picker," she said. "When girls argued about who got to choose teams, you already knew who was going to win." "And who was that?" I asked.

"Those girls everybody liked. They always got to choose. But I didn't care about being liked by everyone." The exchange was short, no more than two minutes, but it spoke volumes. Mary was clearly among the Picked.

Understanding the Picked is one of the more complex aspects of group dynamics. Reflecting on my own childhood, I tend to divide the Picked into two subgroups: those who were consistently chosen (the *Always Picked*), and those who were only picked occasionally (the *Occasionally Picked*), often when there were no other options. Each group carries its own stories and consequences.

Always Picked

The children who were chosen immediately or shortly after team picking began were part of a group I call the *Always Picked*. Teachers and classmates often attributed their quick selection to height, athletic ability, or popularity. These children rarely feared exclusion. They were highly sought after because they possessed traits the Pickers valued. Other children were competing to have them on their team, which often reinforced their sense of self-worth. We will examine how this confidence may stem from intrinsic characteristics, such as height, to extrinsic cultural factors, such as the clothing or shoes children wear.

The only time tension seemed to surface was when an Always Picked child decided they no longer wanted to be picked; they wanted to be in charge. When one of them stepped forward to become a Picker, the social dynamic shifted. While many of them had the raw ability to lead, they were not Pickers by default. Pickers typically brought something more visible: charisma, boldness, or an assertive personality. Still, in moments when not enough Pickers were present, the Always Picked often filled that role by necessity.

This group had talent. They could perform. They were often athletic, capable, and dependable in games like baseball, basketball, hopscotch, or jump rope. But unlike the Pickers, they were often quieter, less visibly assertive, more introverted. What they lacked in showmanship, they often made up for in focus and resilience. Many worked through discomfort, showing up day after day to get incrementally better.

Whether conducting leadership training or teaching college courses, I emphasize that leadership qualities can be developed. Personality tends to form early, but character is shaped through discipline, intentional habits, and reflection. Seasoned educators and trainers understand that our goal is not to simply transfer information, but to cultivate the mind's ability to think critically. This reminds me of something Albert Einstein said in 1921 during a visit to Boston: *"Education is not the learning of facts, but the training of minds to think"* (Butt, 2019, p. 1). That idea feels especially relevant in an era where information is available instantly through digital platforms and search engines. Therefore, a critical idea to consider when educating young minds is that self-confidence can be nurtured.

For the Always Picked, it often begins on the playground, where being consistently chosen sends a powerful message to a child about their worth. With repeated affirmation from peers, many Always Picked children develop a strong sense of self and eventually begin to assert control over the selection process. Over time, they may become Pickers themselves. Through socialization, they learn to expect to be picked first and to associate their identity with that expectation. *Socialization* is the process through which society teaches us about our cultures, our roles, what to believe, and what attitudes, norms, and expectations by which we govern ourselves. These shape the perception of ourselves as we grow (Thompson & Hickey, 2016).

What happens when Always Picked children grow up and bring those expectations into adulthood? In many cases, they arrive in the workplace with a strong sense of entitlement or anticipation, expecting recognition, selection, or advancement. Their swagger often mirrors that of the childhood Pickers.

In my own years of consulting and training, I've observed that competition in the workplace often brings out the worst in people, not the best. We don't refer to our colleagues as collaborators when we're competing; we call them competitors. As Stephen Covey once noted,

> *Competition has its place in the marketplace or against last year's performance, perhaps even against another office or individual, where there is no particular interdependence, no need to cooperate. But cooperation in the workplace is as important to free enterprise as competition in the marketplace. The spirit of Win/Win cannot survive in an environment of competition and contests.*
>
> (Covey, Seven Habits, p. 230)

Pickers and Always Picked children often grow into adults with distinct social traits—traits shaped by early roles and reinforced by years of feedback from peers, teachers, and authority figures. The differences aren't only visible from the outside. They often settle deep into one's personality and sense of self.

Taller children, especially those who carry themselves with confidence, charisma, and assertiveness, are more likely to be "publicly anointed" as leaders. Meanwhile, shorter children, or those who are quieter and less inclined to self-promote, often remain overlooked, regardless of their capability. The question isn't just whether height influences how others see you, but whether it also changes how you see yourself. Our experiences suggest it does. Height, visibility, and early social positioning often determine who gets tapped for leadership, long before leadership is earned.

Research supports this observation. A cross-national analysis by Kortt et al. (2019) found that taller individuals were significantly more likely to hold leadership and management roles, suggesting physical stature itself may be treated as an *implicit* qualification for authority. Another study by Re and Perrett (2014) showed that observers across genders associate greater height with competence, dominance, and leadership potential, even when other factors are held constant.

This bias begins early. In his book *Outliers*, Malcolm Gladwell (2008) illustrates how youth sports leagues often give an edge to children born earlier in the calendar year. Those kids are slightly older, slightly bigger, and, as a result, more likely to be seen as talented. That tiny head start grows into a lasting advantage as they're given more playing time, better coaching, and greater confidence. In some European soccer leagues, there are no professional players born in the last quarter of the year, a staggering reminder that timing and visibility often outweigh raw ability (Merron, 2008).

Consider height again in the context of corporate and political leadership. One survey found that male Fortune 500 CEOs were nearly ten times more likely to be 6' 2" or taller than the average American man (Fleming, 2011). In presidential politics, voters tend to favor the taller candidate. Between 1900 and 2020, the taller candidates won 21 of the 31 US elections, an overwhelming trend with only a few exceptions.

These patterns are subtle but powerful. Socialization teaches us who "looks" like a leader and who doesn't. It sets unconscious standards for confidence, authority, and worthiness. And those standards follow children into adolescence, college, workplace, and boardrooms. As adults, the early messages about who leads and who follows still echo, and they shape who speaks, who gets heard, and who gets chosen.

From early on, boys and girls absorb signals about who they are and what roles are open to them. In many classrooms, boys and girls are still separated during playtime. Teachers, often unknowingly, reinforce differences by appealing to gender norms. We would never dream of saying, "Japanese kids over here, Latino kids over there," but we still say, "Boys and girls, line up in separate rows!" (O'Neil, 2005).

Even brand identities reflect these norms. The Ritz-Carlton's once-proud motto, "Ladies and gentlemen serving ladies and gentlemen," now sounds like something from a fading era. Today, the phrase lands differently. It doesn't reflect a world striving for inclusive leadership and evolving norms, particularly around gender and identity.

Other brands signaled elements of popular culture and perhaps even social and economic class, for instance, in how children dressed among children. I recall a boy in my third-grade class who always wore the latest Converse sneakers. His shoes made him a trendsetter. Other children followed him because he looked the part. From clothes to charisma to confidence, these cues continue to shape how people in adulthood are perceived, picked, and promoted.

This kind of early social conditioning doesn't fade away. It shapes the way individuals experience education, navigate professional environments, and define success. The Recess Effect, in that way, is not just a childhood phenomenon; it continues into adulthood, influencing behavior and expectations across all levels of society.

The children who were Always Picked may have shown the same level of interpersonal skill as the Pickers, but they often lacked the assertiveness or dominance that allowed Pickers to control the selection process. Ironically, the qualities that gave Pickers influence were not always admirable. As discussed earlier, traits such as boldness, social confidence, and strategic self-positioning can secure visibility, but they do not automatically foster inclusion. In some cases, they can undermine it.

As adults, the Always Picked commonly become employees rather than supervisors. However, as we discussed earlier, some who become Always Picked function as supervisors, managers, directors, executives, or owners in their adult lives. These individuals may walk into rooms expecting recognition, praise, or advancement, not based on performance, but on a lifelong belief that being chosen is their default setting. With a childhood history of Always Picked, they possess similar entitled expectations when they become adults in the workplace. They interpret workplace higher-ups not selecting them for assignments, promotions, and the like as unfair. The famous business management author, Dr. Henry Mintzberg, once said, "Confidence without competence breeds arrogance" (Mintzberg, 2005). Studies show that incompetent managers often lack the minimal level of competence required to recognize their own limitations (Luhova et al., 2021).

They often overrate their own abilities and undervalue those around them and behave accordingly. When incompetence is paired with overconfidence and ignorance, the result can be both disruptive and damaging. One could argue that the most dangerous individuals are not those who are simply unskilled, but those who lack the self-awareness to recognize it.

In the same way, those lacking competence rarely recognize the harm they cause; it's their colleagues and teams who bear the weight. Without a baseline level of self-awareness, they mistake their missteps for strength and their failures for misjudgments by others. Research on leadership psychology has long shown that inflated self-perception often masks deeper insecurities. These managers may experience some professional success, at least superficially, but their presence leaves a trail of collateral damage. The costs show up in team morale, productivity, and trust.

Oscar Wilde once said, "Some cause happiness wherever they go; others, whenever they go." His wisecrack, though humorous, captures a hard truth about emotional intelligence in leadership. A mental health professional once shared with me that, after decades of practice, nearly every woman they counseled, despite being widely regarded as beautiful, answered "no" when asked if she believed she was attractive. It's a telling example of how external validation doesn't always lead to self-belief. The same disconnect appears in some men who rise to positions of power, carrying themselves with inflated authority while lacking the clarity or judgment their roles demand.

Both examples speak to the same truth: outward presentation often reveals little about inward strength. And in the workplace, unacknowledged insecurity, especially when masked by ego, can derail even the most talented teams.

Occasionally Picked: Almost a Benchwarmer

One of my co-author's colleagues was among the Always Picked but occasionally was not picked until the very end during recess team selections. She said it was a "horrifying experience" that haunted her for years. She said that she felt like an outcast and not part of the group/class and that these experiences were nothing short of traumatizing. This example brings us to the next group we have classified as the *Occasionally Picked*. On the playground, these are those children who were selected after the Always Picked, the so-called "A-list." Their placement was inconsistent. Some days they made it onto a team early; other days, they waited too long and drifted to the margins. They lived in the in-between.

These children tended to be transient during recess. Often, they would hover near one game or gathering, hoping to be noticed. If they weren't picked quickly, they'd slip away unnoticed to another part of the playground. This wasn't just about playing; it was about managing the sting of being overlooked. By moving around, they increased their chances of inclusion while avoiding the sting of visible rejection.

What set the Occasionally Picked apart was their hustle. They were often the most active group on the playground, not necessarily in the games, but in their determination to stay in motion. They were always scanning, negotiating, or pivoting. They were chameleons, blending where needed, shifting when left out. Their behavior wasn't about apathy. It was about resilience and an enduring desire to belong.

For those only occasionally chosen to join a team, the experience often carried an undercurrent of emotional strain. If you were one of them, you likely remember the knot in your stomach as the Pickers called out names. One colleague I interviewed for this book described that feeling vividly, even though it happened over 50 years ago, back when he was shorter than his peers, a late bloomer in puberty. These moments stay with people. They shape how we see ourselves. For the Occasionally Picked, recess could feel like a high-stakes audition. They weren't always first, but they weren't always overlooked either. They weren't the best at sports, but they could play. Often, they simply wanted to be part of a team, just to be included.

This group often enters the workplace shaped by that experience, contributing steadily but avoiding the spotlight. Their goal wasn't dominance. It was belonging. The Pickers did not fight over them, and that reality, subtle as it may seem, formed the emotional backdrop of their formative years. Even among the Picked, there's a hierarchy, and the Occasionally Picked knew exactly where they stood.

George and David's Story: a Case in Point

> *My personal experience, and that of my childhood friend David, offers another lens on the dynamics of being Picked. In our early school years, both of us were athletic and often among the Always Picked during recess and team-based activities. That shifted around middle school, when most of our peers experienced growth spurts—except us. By high school, we were noticeably shorter than most of our classmates. Despite our ability, we found ourselves less frequently selected and eventually settled into the ranks of the Occasionally Picked. It wasn't until after graduation that we reached our adult heights, 5′9″ for me and 5′11″ for David.*
>
> *David, now a journalist known for holding public officials accountable, once reflected on our shared experience. He noted that spending those years on the sidelines may have shaped our sense of empathy and helped us better understand what it feels like to be overlooked. That reflection has stayed with me, especially as we consider how early experiences influence our adult behaviors and beliefs, not just socially, but professionally.*

In short, our childhood playground experiences fundamentally influence our perceptions of ourselves and touch our respective futures.

The Benchwarmers

Without thoughtful oversight, recess can create stress for some children, especially those who are shy, anxious, or targets of bullying (Mader, 2023). I witnessed this firsthand during my older daughter's fifth-grade year.

One afternoon, I arrived early to pick her up and stood by the fence watching the children play. A group of boys was organizing a basketball game. Two boys stood in the middle, clearly serving as Pickers. About nine other boys surrounded them, waiting to be picked. The process began as one of the Pickers pointed and said, "I want Tom." Tom then moved behind him. The other Picker responded, "I'll take Sam," and Sam took his place. One by one, boys were selected. As the game of picking continued, seven boys remained. You could feel the tension in their body language, nervous fidgeting, eyes shifting, or hands in pockets. Four more were eventually selected, visibly relieved as they joined their teams. That left three boys unpicked. Two of them sat on the nearby picnic table to watch, clearly disappointed. The third boy drifted toward the playground, alone. How did they feel as they waited? Only those who have stood in that uncertain line can fully relate to the mix of hope, embarrassment, and dread that moment holds. It reminded me of my own days at recess, and it was a powerful example of what we call The Recess Effect.

Later, I asked my daughter about those boys. She recognized them and explained that while they weren't always excluded, they were often chosen late, what we categorize as Occasionally Picked. That day just wasn't their day. Interestingly, she then pointed out another child on the field, one who wasn't even in the basketball group. "They never pick him," she said, "unless the teacher makes them." He had chosen instead to chase squirrels by himself. We'll return to that boy later as we explore the plight of Benchwarmers. But the scene brought clarity to how the Occasionally Picked live in between, neither Always Picked nor full Benchwarmers, but vulnerable to either outcome.

As adults, the Occasionally Picked often become one of the most complex workplace profiles. Almost like Lobbyists. Their formative years taught them to advocate for themselves, sometimes subtly, sometimes forcefully, just to be seen. Over time, those efforts shape their approach to work. They may become intensely driven, hyper-competitive, or more strategic about positioning.

This group often learned negotiation early, not through formal training, but through the experience of needing to persuade others for inclusion. That instinct can morph into a "do whatever it takes" mentality that plays out in professional settings. They want to prove their worth, sometimes at the expense of collaboration, fairness, or patience. Workplace literature often highlights competitive or overly political employees but rarely explores where those tendencies come from. We believe unpacking The Recess Effect provides that missing link.

Think back. Can you remember the children who were always trying to join the group? The ones hanging close, hoping for an invitation? The Occasionally Picked weren't looking for popularity; they just wanted to play, to belong. But belonging came inconsistently, and the effort to gain it became exhausting. These were the children who may have said, almost under their breath, "Please pick me," or "Can I play?" not once, but often. That emotional labor leaves a mark. As adults, some continue to seek validation from authority figures, interpreting professional recognition as long-overdue affirmation. If you have never noticed these interactions on the playground, you might consider observing recess at a local elementary school. You'll likely see the patterns: some children gathered in the center, others hovering at the edges, and a few standing completely alone. These social dynamics are not just childhood memories; they are often blueprints for adulthood.

The Recess Effect proposes that as children mature, they repeat elementary school playground dynamics throughout high school, college, and eventually the workplace. Human beings are adaptive, but adaptation doesn't always lead to healthy outcomes. Sadly, children who were Occasionally Picked often grow up carrying emotional residue from years spent on the margins. They may internalize rejection, envy, or a persistent fear of being left out. What can we expect from children who spend so much of their early lives striving to belong? Some develop an intense resentment toward their Always Picked peers or the Pickers who once had the power to choose. That resentment can evolve. In some cases, the same individuals who once felt excluded adopt controlling or domineering behaviors as adults—not because they were always powerful, but because they once felt powerless. Research has shown that experiences of social exclusion and childhood marginalization are linked to later aggressive or retaliatory behaviors in adult settings, including workplace bullying (Salmivalli & Peets, 2009; Coyne et al., 2000).

A college classmate, Harold, once told me he never had a friend in high school. I was stunned. He struck me as kind, thoughtful, and easy to like. I asked how that was possible. Harold explained that, growing up, he spent most of his time "playing up" to the popular kids, and that very effort, ironically, kept him from forming real friendships.

Like many of us, Harold faced challenges more than once in his youth. He said the kids he tried to befriend set impossibly high expectations. Coming from a financially modest family, he wore hand-me-downs from older siblings, especially, as he put it, "those old shoes." He was often judged for what he lacked, not for who he was. He wasn't athletic, and he envied those who were.

Still, Harold learned how to blend in. He said it was all performance. Even his own family believed he was popular, assuming he was having fun at school. But behind the scenes, Harold operated with a focused, deliberate presence. He was fiercely competitive, willing to say or do what it took to meet his goals. He knew how to play social games. Like the Picked, he mimicked loyalty to the Pickers, masking the careful calculation behind his every move. And like the Picked, he distanced himself from the Benchwarmers.

Harold's story illustrates the inner world of the Occasionally Picked. They navigate adolescence with calculation, working hard to secure a spot, yet never quite feeling like they belong. Their social agility masks a deeper insecurity, one that leaves lasting impressions long after recess ends.

Frank's Story: a Case in Point

George Alexakis's neighbor, Frank, told him how he was always the last to be picked. "I was 5'11" but skinny," he explained. He appeared athletic, but he was not. Therefore, Pickers selected him with high expectations, but he could not follow through athletically. He eventually ended up in a pattern of the Pickers choosing him last. He said, "I hated it!" He strongly believes that this influenced his social and professional life until this day. Now in his 60s, he has had the same five friends since high school. When attending parties, he experiences anxiety about whom he will talk to and often looks for someone that is similar to him. Although he is a kind person, his asocial tendencies limit his interactions; he only converses with my co-author among all the neighbors and just waves to the rest. People sometimes view him as indifferent or irate in professional settings, even though he is not. They often erroneously believe that he does not like them because of his demeanor. Frank attributes all of his social challenges mainly to the playground childhood exclusions.

A Benchwarmer's Tale: Silence, Withdrawal, and Lost Potential

Remember the old adage, "Sticks and stones can break your bones, but words will never hurt you?" This falsehood reinforces one of the many misconceptions that children have been led to believe in. I recall a fifth-grade elementary school experience regarding a classmate named Eric Beheaven. Children can be unkind, and Eric was usually on the receiving end of their cruelty. The other children often called him "Weird Eric" and other names that were quite piercing and hurtful. Despite the treatment that he experienced, Eric tried to participate in recess activities. He possessed all the qualities that would make Pickers overlook him. He was physically small. He was soft-spoken. He was not athletic. Eric walked with a slight limp, which made him an easy target for teasing and often overlooked during team selection. Even so, Eric would attempt to join an activity where team selection was happening. The Pickers simply did not pick him. Worse, they would very frequently make derogatory remarks about him in front of all the other children.

Eric, then, belongs to the category of Benchwarmers, those routinely left out when teams were chosen. These children were often passed over without acknowledgment, left to navigate recess alone while others played. You could see it in their eyes, a look of resignation that settled in during selection time. Despite the public nature of picking, little in academic or popular literature has seriously explored what it means to be consistently excluded. This chapter turns toward that silence. It examines not only the emotional toll of exclusion, but also the lasting power of words. It invites reflection on the harmful labels and offhand remarks that Benchwarmers absorbed and carried with them long after childhood ended.

Words wound in ways that physical injuries rarely do. Bruises fade and bones heal, but spoken cruelty often leaves scars that linger long after the moment has passed. Emotional injuries can be harder to detect and far more difficult to repair. Research suggests that sustained negative emotional states may even contribute to cellular damage in the body (Sadeghi, 2018). In short, words carry power, and that power can shape lives.

Many adults struggle with depression rooted not in recent events, but in painful childhood experiences from which they never fully recovered. This is not speculation. Children who are teased, isolated, or bullied during their formative years face higher risks of long-term academic, social, and health challenges. These outcomes are not coincidental. Isolated children are also disproportionately vulnerable to exploitation (Arévalo et al., 2014; van Dam, 2001).

I began noticing Eric in third grade. By sixth grade, he had changed profoundly. For years, he tried to fit in. Eventually, he stopped trying. Not only was he routinely overlooked during recess, but he became the target of ridicule from both the Pickers and the Picked. Mockery replaced indifference, and the light from Eric's spirit seemed to slowly dim. He began spending recess alone. Then he started talking to himself aloud. To the other children, he became "the strange kid." Girls would whisper, "Stay away from Freaky Eric; he's weird."

What can we expect from children whose circumstances push them toward isolation rather than inclusion? When the instinct to belong is repeatedly met with rejection, some children reverse course altogether. Mental health professionals refer to this as *reaction formation* (McLeod, 2024): abandoning the desire for acceptance and moving deliberately in the opposite direction.

What I remember most about Eric is how his outward eccentricities intensified each year. The emotional strain of the Recess Effect became more than he could bear. His physical and social distance from other children widened steadily. By third grade, he exhibited many traits common among Benchwarmers: he was quiet, awkward, and unsure of himself. Eventually, he stopped asking to join games at all.

Eric turned inward. During recess, he read comic books while others played. He walked the far edges of the playground, reading aloud softly or speaking to himself. Over time, his interest in comics deepened into obsession. He began acting out scenes, running wildly, pretending to fly or fight unseen enemies. Teachers and classmates left him alone. He was not the only child who did.

By sixth grade, Eric's appearance changed. He wore dark clothes, heavy boots, belts, and black shirts. By ninth grade, he had found others who shared his style and interests. What we later came to know as Goth culture was unfamiliar to us at the time, and we didn't yet understand its appeal. While research does not support simplistic links between Goth culture and violence, studies have found a longitudinal relationship between Goth self-identification and depression, self-harm, and suicide attempts (Bogt et al., 2020). The culture did not cause these struggles, but it offered a home for those already carrying them.

Eric also turned to numbing behaviors, including alcohol and drugs, alongside peers who shared his lifestyle. He harbored deep resentment toward those who had rejected him and isolated himself further from anyone outside his circle. I don't know what became of Eric. What I do know is that I never saw him smile after third grade. He seemed perpetually burdened, his demeanor darkened by years of unspoken suffering.

Eric is one of the few people whose fate has stayed with me long after childhood. His story reflects how chronic emotional pain, once visible and acute, can become normalized and invisible over time. What begins as playground exclusion can harden into lifelong scars.

Many people share experiences like Eric's. Most of us can remember a child like him. The consequences of the Recess Effect for Benchwarmers are not fleeting. The internal conflict formed in those early years often emerges later like withdrawal, rebellion, or rejection of the very systems that rejected them. In Eric's case, his childhood experiences of the Recess Effect may have acted as a catalyst.

Learning from Stories of those Affected by the Recess Effect

We can all likely identify with one of the three primary roles on the playground: Picker, Picked, or Benchwarmer. Whether or not we thought about it at the time, many of us lived through similar moments. And we still carry the impact. Those early experiences often shape how we interact with others later in life, especially in the workplace. They can also manifest in our personal relationships beyond it. Over more than a decade of writing this book, my coauthors and I have asked countless people which group they belonged to. Nearly everyone remembered being a Picker or a Picked. Almost no one initially recalled anyone in the third group, unless they themselves had been a Benchwarmer.

Benchwarmers represent those who were rarely, if ever, chosen during childhood games, and often remain unseen in adulthood despite their potential. We hope to challenge the notion that people who appear to live on the margins of society are innately incapable of stepping up to the challenges posed to them in life, whether this ineptitude manifested while they were in school or as they transition to the adult workplace. Just as being characterized as a benchwarmer is not an innate characteristic, leadership is not innate either. Both characteristics are derived from socialization. Thus, exclusion can suppress, but not erase, capacity.

The workplace often mirrors these early exclusions, relegating some people to roles far below their capabilities. However, the Benchwarmers' stories also reveal incredible resilience, empathy, and insight. When given support and space, these individuals can become some of the most impactful leaders. Thus, in the next chapter, we turn our attention to The Apple Effect as a counter to The Recess Effect. We will therefore explore ways for everyone to break away from the mental schemas we form of others that prevent us from seeing the full potential of our colleagues.

References

Arévalo, E., Chavira, D., Cooper, B., & Smith, M. (2014). *SAFE (Screening Applicants for Effectiveness): Guidelines to prevent child molestation in mentoring and youth-serving organizations*. Friends for Youth Inc.

Bogt, T. F. M., Gabhainn, S. N., Simons-Morton, B. G., Ferreira, M., Hublet, A., & Godeau, E. (2020). Goth music and depressive symptoms among adolescents: A longitudinal study. *Journal of Youth and Adolescence, 49*(1), 181–194.

Butt, G. (2019). *Exploring education studies*. Routledge.

Covey, S. R. (1989). *The 7 habits of highly effective people: Powerful lessons in personal change*. Free Press.

Coyne, I., Seigne, E., & Randall, P. (2000). Predicting workplace victim status from personality. *European Journal of Work and Organizational Psychology, 9*(3), 335–349.

Fleming, G. (2011). The height of success. *The Economist*. https://www.economist.com.

Gladwell, M. (2008). *Outliers: The story of success*. Little, Brown and Company.

Kortt, M. A., Leigh, A., & Dollery, B. (2019). Height, leadership and earnings: A cross-national analysis. *Economics and Human Biology, 34,* 1–12.

Luhova, H., Serikov, Y., Liutviieva, S., Serikova, I., & Kovalova, O. (2021). Professional competence and individual-psychological characteristics of managers. *Global Journal of Guidance and Counseling: Theory and Practice, 11*(2), 114–125. https://doi.org/10.18844/gjgc.v11i2.5473.

Mader, J. (2023, October 2). The complicated business of making sure every kid has a great recess. *The Hechinger Report*. https://hechingerreport.org.
McLeod, S. (2024, January 24). Reaction formation: Defense mechanism in psychology. *Simply Psychology*. https://www.simplypsychology.org.
Merron, J. (2008). Relative age effect in European soccer. *European Sport Management Quarterly*, *8*(3), 279–298.
Mintzberg, H. (2005). *Managers not MBAs: A hard look at the soft practice of managing and management development*. Berrett-Koehler Publishers. https://mintzberg.org/books/managers-not-mbas.
O'Neil, J. (2005). The myth of pink and blue brains: A conversation with Lise Eliot. *Educational Leadership*, *63*(1). https://doi.org/10.4135/9781446247143.n5.
Re, D. E., & Perrett, D. I. (2014). The effects of facial adiposity on attractiveness and perceived leadership ability. *Biology Letters*, *10*(4), 20140120.
Sadeghi, H. (2018). *The clarity cleanse: 12 steps to finding renewed energy, spiritual fulfillment, and emotional healing*. Grand Central Life & Style.
Salmivalli, C., & Peets, K. (2009). Bullies, victims, and bully-victim relationships in middle childhood and early adolescence. In K. H. Rubin, W. M. Bukowski, & B. Laursen (Eds.), *Handbook of peer interactions, relationships, and groups* (pp. 322–340). Guilford Press.
Thompson, W. E., & Hickey, J. V. (2016). *Society in focus: An introduction to sociology* (8th ed.). Rowman & Littlefield.
van Dam, C. (2001). *Identifying child molesters: Preventing child sexual abuse by recognizing the patterns of the offenders*. Haworth Maltreatment & Trauma Press.

5

The Apple Effect

Looking Beyond the Surface

Choosing Beyond the Surface

I was once called in to mediate a tense conflict between members of two departments at a university; each convinced the other was to blame for the underperformance of a shared program. Tensions had simmered for months. By the time I entered the scene, each side was convinced the other was to blame, each expecting the other to be corrected. No one was expecting transformation. That's precisely what made the next step so critical.

On the first day of our mediated session, I invited all stakeholders into the same room. They arrived early, looking guarded, eyes full of skepticism, files in hand, faces tight, and postures stiff. You could feel the defensiveness hovering in the air, like a fog of unresolved grievances. I greeted each person with a handshake and a smile, then walked to the front of the room and offered them something they didn't expect: a story.

I asked them to take a deep breath and picture themselves walking into a grocery store. Not just any errand, but a leisurely visit to the produce section, no distractions, no checklist. Just a moment to browse. *"Think of the apples," I said. "Rows of them stacked like polished gems; red, golden, green. Now walk slowly past*

DOI: 10.4324/9781003752219-5

the varieties until you find the red ones. Go ahead, reach for the biggest, brightest, most beautiful red apple you see." They nodded, some smirked. *"You've done this before,"* I *continued. "We all have. Now imagine taking that apple home. You can't wait to bite into it. But this time, just before you do, you slice it open, and inside, it's brown. Mealy. Bruised to the core."* Silence. I paused, letting the image land. *"Have you ever brought home a perfect-looking apple that turned out to be disappointing on the inside?"*

Now I had them.*"Here's the twist," I said. "Some of the best-tasting apples I've ever eaten didn't look like much at all. A little dull. A little odd-shaped. But once I gave them a chance, once I stopped judging by the surface, they turned out to be exceptional."* Heads began to tilt. Arms relaxed. They were listening. *"And that,"* I concluded, *"is what I call the Apple Effect. We often judge people the same way we judge fruit, by what's shiny, familiar, or polished on the outside. But if we want to build something truly excellent, we have to stop picking teams based on the surface. We need to get better at recognizing depth, character, and value beneath the peel."* That metaphor stayed with the group through the entire session. *The Apple Effect* isn't really about fruit. It's about perception. It's about the way we're conditioned, often from childhood, to equate surface appeal with value. And how that conditioning keeps us from recognizing excellence when it doesn't look the way we expect.

The Apple Effect in Action

The Apple Effect parallels the old adage, "You can't judge a book by its cover," but applied to human potential, it cuts even deeper. We often make snap judgments based on appearance, confusing polish for promise, charisma for character, and confidence for competence. Yet, just as some of the most delicious apples never make it to the produce shelves because of surface blemishes, people with remarkable talents are regularly overlooked for reasons that have nothing to do with their ability to contribute.

There's a surprising truth in nature that illustrates this: apples with slight discoloration, caused by a harmless fungus, actually ramp up their antioxidant production as a defense mechanism, making them sweeter, more nutritious, and healthier than their flawless counterparts (Griffith & Griffith, 2024). It's more than a metaphor; it's a reminder of how we should rethink our biases when evaluating people.

One of my co-authors recalled a moment from an early Apple company documentary that stood out, not because of the products, but because of the people. Among the engineers and leaders featured in the film was a woman who didn't fit the polished executive image so common in corporate America at the time. She was candid, capable, and quite competent, but in an era where leadership often came wrapped in a narrow mold—tall, white, male, country-club-ready—she stood apart.

What made her presence remarkable wasn't just that she had defied stereotypes, but that Apple had clearly hired her for the right reasons: her intelligence, her operational skills, and her ability to deliver results. She mentioned, without bitterness, how rare it was to receive such an opportunity in a field that so often judged candidates by how they looked before considering what they could offer. In that moment, the company, Apple, demonstrated the kind of thinking this chapter encourages: choosing substance over surface appearance.

That moment wasn't about tokenism or optics; it was about recognizing brilliance where others might overlook it. Apple didn't just break convention in its products. In its early days, it challenged assumptions about who belonged in the room. That is the essence of the Apple Effect: looking beyond the gloss to find the core.

That story helped anchor the concept when I introduced the Apple Effect to the two university departments tasked with resolving a cross-departmental standoff. As I walked them through the metaphor, they softened. They saw themselves in it, not just the bruises, but the sweetness beneath. That clarity opened the door to a new way of working together, grounded in authenticity and potential. We moved forward with a clear process: First, we asked the hard question: What's really going on here? Not the noise, missed emails, overlapping roles, or unclear directives, but the root causes. What were the underlying frustrations? The real causes of mistrust? Teams are like families in that way; problems rarely come from where they appear to. Misdiagnosing the issue would only land us back at the beginning in six months.

Once we identified the root causes, we stepped back to consider the broader picture. I encouraged them to see the organization not as two departments, but as a living system. Nothing happens in isolation. A breakdown in one area often reflects strain somewhere else. This way of thinking, what some call "systems thinking," allowed us to reframe the problem (World Economic Forum, 2021). One person joked that the approach felt like jumping from a maze to a mountain view. Even the boldest suggestions were now on the table. Instead of resisting them, people leaned in.

From there, we co-created a working plan. This wasn't about who had the loudest voice or the highest title (an early ground rule we established was that everyone had to check their titles at the door). Everyone had a role, everyone had ownership, and the timeline wasn't imposed; it was agreed upon. When people feel heard, they engage. And when they engage, they deliver.

The final step, too often skipped, was follow-through. We didn't walk away after signing off. Both teams agreed to stay in communication and revisit progress regularly. That commitment made all the difference. Today, that very program is still thriving, and internally, they refer to it as "the Apple Effect project."

Here's the reality behind the metaphor: our worth doesn't fluctuate with our wardrobe. Whether we walk into a store in sneakers and shorts or a tailored suit, the core of who we are remains the same. But the treatment we receive? That often hinges on how we're packaged. The saying "perception is reality" may be a cultural reflex, but it's also a convenient lie. Perception isn't reality; it's just a filtered lens, shaped by bias, comfort, and assumption.

When we mistake perception for truth, we build cultures that reward the familiar over the exceptional, the polished over the capable. We sideline those who don't fit the mold, not because they lack value, but because we never bothered to look deeper. And in doing so, we don't just miss out on talent. We teach people to shrink themselves, to armor up, and to conform. The real cost?

Innovation withers, morale erodes, and entire ecosystems of brilliance go undiscovered.

The Apple Effect dares us to break that cycle. It invites us to choose curiosity over comfort and take a chance on undiscovered talent in our workplaces. One company put it best in a recent job posting: *"We don't just hire people who mirror our culture. We hire people who add to it"* (National Credit Care, 2023). That's the Apple Effect in action.

From Picker to Manager: The Apple Effect versus The Recess Effect

The spotlight on leaders today is unrelenting, but not because they're expected to have all the answers. It's because the questions keep changing. In a world where information floods every corner of the workplace, clarity is scarce. Priorities collide. Stakeholders demand authenticity and agility at the same time. And the ground beneath what used to be considered "good leadership" has shifted; steadily and, in some cases, radically. The people doing the work want something more grounded:

Figure 5.1 presents the leadership expectations that emerged most prominently from contributor experiences. Participants emphasized the importance of visible values, courageous conversations, protection of diverse perspectives, and a distinction between mere compliance and true excellence. Collectively, these expectations underscore the critical role leaders play in shaping environments where individuals feel seen, heard, respected, and empowered to contribute fully.

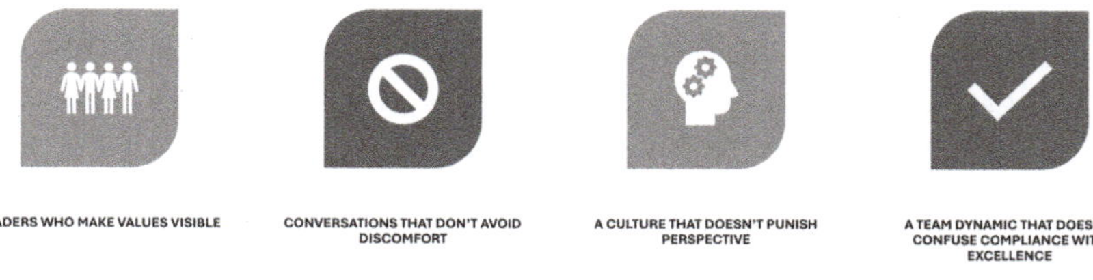

FIGURE 5.1 Key Leadership Expectations

What defines effective leadership now isn't a checklist of competencies. It's the ability to hold people together when pressure, personality, and competing priorities threaten to pull them apart. Conflict stems not just from cultural gaps but from differing communication styles, generational lenses, and values. Authority no longer earns automatic trust. A title doesn't secure influence. Even strong performance doesn't guarantee loyalty. The people doing the work want something deeper. More grounded. More real.

This chapter explores why the old ways of selecting and promoting leaders, shaped in part by playground instincts, no longer serve us. It's not enough to look the part. Today, substance matters more than polish. Depth matters more than charisma. In this era of AI acceleration and increased transparency, organizations can't afford surface-level leadership. They need leaders who foster psychological safety.

Psychological safety, a term discussed in Amy Edmondson's work, *The Fearless Organization: Creating Psychological Safety in the Workplace for Learning, Innovation, and Growth* (2018; Edmondson & Kerrissey, 2025), speaks to leaders developing environments where their employees feel safe to speak up and share ideas about what is going wrong and how they might improve things. It is not about being 'nice' but instead, sharing important truths by speaking up and having constructive, candid, and respectful debates about workplace situations, processes, products or services to avoid costly mistakes down the line. In teams where psychological safety is prioritized, leaders in organizations understand that their teams are going to make mistakes; they might even bet on it! Thus, they cultivate an environment where their teams are allowed to experiment and make mistakes, and as Peter Sims proposed, *fail forward*, so that they can learn how to improve the work that they do, without risking denigration or retribution due to perceived lost time or money (Sims, 2011).

They also need colleagues who bring substance, empathy, problem-solving, ethics, and critical thinking to the center of the work. And that substance isn't declared. It's felt. This, too, is the Apple Effect at work.

The Apple Effect is the ability to look past surface-level polish and recognize the deeper values, capabilities, and integrity that drive lasting leadership and organizational health. These aren't "nice-to-haves," they're survival-level competencies in a time when public scrutiny is constant, political pressures are shifting, and employees are less tolerant of performance without purpose. "Pretending" is losing its place.

And as expectations evolve, so does our definition of leadership. Most people can recall a leader who inspired them, someone who helped them discover alignment between their personal values and a collective vision. The best leaders don't push people into compliance; they ignite something in them. These leaders can disappear from the room, and the work keeps thriving. That's not charisma, it's values in motion. Yet, for all our talk about values-based leadership, many still struggle to name a manager who actually embodies it. The Apple Effect in leadership occurs when leaders demonstrate visible expressions of leadership but equally demonstrate their values (their sense of right and wrong) by their actions. The outside reflects the inside for highly evolved leaders. They display actions, indicating that they always seek to do the right thing personally and professionally with qualities of honesty, fairness, integrity, and openness (Brown & Treviño, 2006).

Too often, leadership becomes a performance. Individuals ascend to management because they appear the part: articulate, confident, and persuasive. The handshake is firm. The tone is serious. The image is curated. But substance doesn't always follow.

One of my co-authors recalls a coach at his university who was hired, in part, because of how perfectly he projected leadership. Seemingly, the height, the voice, the posture, all aligned. But after two years of consistent mismanagement, he was quietly let go. The truth was that this coach hadn't even earned the degree listed on his resume. The image had outpaced the impact. That's not an isolated case. In fact, oral communication remains the most sought-after skill in new hires and has been for decades. Research affirms that which corporations continually express to college and university graduates for the last 50 years: oral communication remains the most highly requested skill that organizations seek and value in managers (Rios et al., 2020). That tells us a lot about what organizations say they value.

The Recess Effect, however, conditions us to look for external cues. Who fits in? Who plays the part? That early training teaches us to favor those who shine publicly, even when substance is lacking. We grow up selecting captains based on confidence, not character. That dynamic continues into the workplace, where those with polished communication styles often rise, even if their core values don't match the mission. But truly great leaders, those guided by what we're calling the Apple Effect, don't just look the part. They live it. They embody humility, fairness, honesty, and integrity, not just in speech but in action. And that consistency matters. While charisma may impress in the short term, values sustain trust over time. Here's where it gets slippery. Many of the values promoted in organizations today are easy to fake. Pride masquerades as passion. Dislike gets branded as tolerance. The word "humility" shows up in award speeches from people basking in applause. However, the workplace is filled with statements of value that aren't backed by behavior.

Tolerance, in particular, has become a comfortable word for many leaders. But tolerance isn't the same as acceptance. It isn't appreciation. It isn't respect. Tolerance says, "I can endure your presence." That's a low bar. When organizations settle there, the environment becomes one of resignation, not belonging. This is how the Recess Effect creeps back in. People who challenge norms or introduce unfamiliar ideas are often labeled "difficult," "not a culture fit," or worse, "uncooperative." Many employees do not disengage because they lack commitment, but because they recognize the familiar warning signs. Speaking up carries consequences. Questioning norms feels unsafe. Remaining silent becomes the adult equivalent of standing on the edge of the playground, watching others play, hoping not to draw attention. Some are pushed out without acknowledgment. Their departures are cloaked in vague emails they'll never see, their access revoked. Truth-telling, especially when principled, is often punished.

This dynamic plays out across sectors. In many cases, conflict-averse managers avoid hard conversations. Instead of addressing underperformance directly, they let it fester, talk around it with others, and then offload it into formal reviews. That avoidance ripples. Others see it. They follow suit. Candor erodes. Trust breaks down. Awkwardness becomes an excuse for inaction. And that's a problem. Grown-up leadership doesn't run from discomfort. It moves toward it with courage, clarity, and care. Avoiding confrontation isn't kindness; it's neglect.

When leaders don't address issues head-on, they create a vacuum where team dynamics erode. People stop trusting each other. The organization's energy drains into managing dysfunction instead of delivering impact. And eventually, what was avoided becomes unmanageable. Leadership isn't always loud. But quietness doesn't always mean wisdom either, as not all quiet leaders are wise. Some are simply evasive. And that evasiveness can mask deeper issues such as indecision, needing to exert control, and insecurity. Micromanagement, for instance, often stems from fear, not excellence. Endless reporting, the constant need for meetings, tracking, and documentation are signs of a leader trying to prove that they are in control rather than cultivate inclusive values.

We've seen this across industries: managers who equate control with effectiveness often carry unresolved personal baggage shaped by exclusion, perfectionism, or fear, and they end up projecting those patterns into their teams. Some never move past the recess yard. Their fixation on dominance, visibility, or affirmation stems from early experiences. The Recess Effect didn't just shape them; it defined how they manage others.

One co-author describes a former administrator as "an intelligent incompetent with an inferiority complex." He didn't shout. He didn't insult. But he withheld promotions for years, not because of merit, but because of ego. When he finally exited the organization where he worked, long-overdue advancements happened within months. His values, shaped by insecurity and masked with polish, left a long shadow.

This man wasn't ineffective because he lacked intellect. He was ineffective because his values were rooted in insecurity and ego, moving counter to the mission. And people felt it. They still talk about him years later, not for what he built, but for what he damaged.

That's the Apple Effect in action: what's underneath always rises. Leadership isn't declared. It's detected. How leaders make decisions, how they treat people when no one's watching, and how they handle power; these things reveal what drives them.

People can't always articulate what feels off in a team or culture. But they sense it: in who gets airtime, who gets heard, who's protected, and who's punished. They know when leadership is rooted in values that build up the team, and when it's not.

The *Recess Effect* encourages us to follow appearances, protect cliques, and avoid disruption. The *Apple Effect* urges us to dig deeper. It invites us to ask not only who is leading, but how and why.

Figure 5.2 illustrates how when teachers serve as coaches during playground activities, the Apple Effect is facilitated. The Apple Effect is the antidote to the Recess Effect. If the Recess Effect taught us to chase the outward appearance, the Apple Effect teaches us to recognize principled conviction. It urges us to stop selecting leaders and teammates the way kids pick players at recess: based on charm, appearance, or familiarity. Instead, we're challenged to recognize the people whose internal qualities, like

FIGURE 5.2 The Apple Effect

Artwork by Claire Rice.

integrity, humility, honesty, and moral courage, coupled with the skill set needed for the positions, make them the steady, ethical forces organizations actually need. The Apple Effect is about learning to spot substance beneath the surface and to choose the person who might not shine at first glance (based on our view of what shiny looks like), but whose actions build trust, whose presence creates safety, and whose values align with something deeper than optics. It invites a reset: to value the bruised apple that's rich with flavor over the flawless one that's mealy inside.

The truth is, we don't just inherit the Recess Effect; we absorb it. It shapes who we admire, who we promote, and who we protect. But we're not stuck with it. Kahneman's work on system one thinking reinforces how we make fast, surface-level judgments that often guide promotions and leadership selections, fitting the Recess Effect perfectly (Kahneman, 2011). The Apple Effect gives us a clearer lens, one that helps us see beyond polish to substance. It offers language, vision, and a path forward. It calls us to lead from the inside out: steady, self-aware, and guided by values. And yet, even as we embrace this more conscious approach to leadership, we must remain alert. Because not every apple is merely bruised; some are rotten to the core. And when that rot goes unchecked, it spreads.

Embracing The Apple Effect: Some Takeaways

The Recess Effect operates by default unless it is deliberately interrupted. It is a conditioning force, formed early and woven into adulthood unconsciously as a habit. From a young age, we learn to scan for visibility, confidence, and familiarity, and to equate those traits with worth. We learn to choose quickly, publicly, and often defensively. Over time, those habits follow us into adulthood, shaping who we trust, who we promote, and who we align with.

The Apple Effect stands in direct contrast. It explains how a different lens can change not only perception but outcomes. Unlike the Recess Effect, it is not automatic. It requires intention. Where the Recess Effect rewards outward cues and speed, the

Apple Effect demands pause, attention, and discernment. It asks leaders to look past outward appearance and examine values, consistency, and character instead. One relies on instinct. The other requires judgment. And while the Recess Effect explains why leadership patterns repeat themselves, the Apple Effect offers a way to interrupt them.

The Apple Effect invites us to see more clearly, but clarity alone is not enough. Recognizing substance beneath appearance is only the beginning. Once leaders learn to pause, look deeper, and choose based on values along with the appropriate skill set, rather than outward appearance, a harder responsibility follows: deciding what they will no longer excuse. Some patterns persist because they are protected. Some behaviors spread because they are rewarded. And some cultures fail not from ignorance but from tolerance of what quietly corrodes trust, judgment, and integrity. As we move forward, the question is no longer whether we can see the difference between what looks right and what actually is. The question is whether we are willing to act when discernment reveals something we would rather ignore. That is where recovery truly begins.

References

Brown, M. E., & Treviño, L. K. (2006). Ethical leadership: A review and future directions. *The Leadership Quarterly, 17*(6), 595–616. https://doi.org/10.1016/j.leaqua.2006.10.004.

Edmondson, A. C. (2018). *The fearless organization: Creating psychological safety in the workplace for learning, innovation, and growth*. Wiley.

Edmondson, A. C., & Kerrissey, M. J. (2025). What people get wrong about psychological safety. *Harvard Business Review, 103*(3), 52–59.

Griffith, A., & Griffith, J. (2024). The antioxidant response of cosmetically blemished apples. *Journal of Food Science & Nutrition, 12*(2), 115–123.

Kahneman, D. (2011). *Thinking, fast and slow*. Farrar, Straus and Giroux.

National Credit Care. (2023). *Client service representative* [Job posting]. National Credit Care Careers.

Rios, D., Ling, C., Pugh, R., Becker, D., & Bacall, A. (2020). Identifying critical 21st-century communication skills for workplace success: A review of employer expectations. *Business and Professional Communication Quarterly*, *83*(2), 163–184. https://doi.org/10.1177/2329490620905464.

Sims, P. (2011). *Little bets: How breakthrough ideas emerge from small discoveries*. Free Press.

World Economic Forum. (2021). Why systems thinking is essential for solving complex global challenges. https://www.weforum.org.

6

When Leadership Perpetuates Playground Dynamics

The Apple Effect offers a way forward beyond the Recess Effect, but it does not guarantee that we course-correct entirely. Even organizations that talk openly about values, ethics, and leadership development are not immune to failure. In fact, some of the most visible organizational collapses in recent history occurred in places that proudly displayed mission statements, conducted ethics training, and promoted strong leadership rhetoric. The problem is not a lack of language. It is a lack of alignment between what is said, what is rewarded, and what is tolerated.

Recovering from the Recess Effect requires more than awareness. It requires vigilance because, without intervention, leadership simply reenacts the same dynamics in more sophisticated settings. While some leadership failures are rooted in immaturity or unconscious conditioning, others emerge from something more dangerous: systems that reward harm, protect power, and normalize behavior that contradicts stated values. This is where the Apple Effect is tested.

DOI: 10.4324/9781003752219-6

When Values and Incentives Diverge

The Apple Effect teaches us to look beneath what's immediately apparent and evaluate leadership by integrity, consistency, and action. But what happens when those deeper values are compromised not by ignorance, but by pressure? What happens when conformity is rewarded more than courage, when results matter more than responsibility, and when "fitting in" becomes a prerequisite for survival? At that point, the issue is no longer who looks like a good leader. The issue is what the organization has become willing to excuse. Much of what we label as individual failure is, in fact, cultural permission. Leaders rarely act in isolation. They operate within incentive structures, peer expectations, and unspoken rules that shape behavior over time. When those forces reward compliance over conscience, even well-intentioned people can drift far from their stated values.

This chapter examines what happens when organizational culture corrodes discernment, when ethical shortcuts are justified as necessities, and when leadership failure spreads not because people are malicious, but because the environment makes integrity costly. The Recess Effect explains how unhealthy patterns take root while the Apple Effect explains how to go beyond facades to recognize the content and substance of one's character. This chapter confronts what happens when neither is enough unless leaders are willing to intervene. Similarly, recovery, as it turns out, is not just about seeing clearly. It's about deciding what will no longer be tolerated.

Chapter 5 asked us to look more closely. This chapter asks us to look more honestly. Because even when leaders recognize the difference between appearance and character, many organizations still reward the wrong things. Over time, those rewards don't just shape behavior, they reshape judgment. What begins as compromise hardens into habit. What was once tolerated becomes expected. And eventually, distortion feels normal. This chapter is not about the wrong behaviors people adopt in the workplace. It is about systems that make good people complicit by silencing principled resistance and rewarding outcomes detached from integrity.

How Good People Drift

I have never met a kindergartener who aspired to fail. Under the right conditions: clear expectations, encouragement, structure, and care, children rise. The same is true of college students. On the first day of class, most arrive hoping to succeed, not to stumble. And in the workplace, I have yet to meet an employee who begins a new job hoping to disappoint others. Most people want to do well. Most want to contribute. Most want to be proud of their work.

But what happens when those conditions gradually begin to shift?

A few years ago, a mid-level director confided in me after a leadership retreat I facilitated. When she first joined her organization, she had a reputation for asking hard questions. In meetings, she would raise concerns about timelines, staffing assumptions, or whether a decision aligned with the company's stated values. At first, her candor was praised. She was described as thoughtful and strategic.

Over time, however, the tone changed. She began to hear comments like, "We need to be careful not to slow things down," or "Let's not overcomplicate this." No one reprimanded her directly. No policy changed. But she noticed she was invited to fewer informal conversations. Her ideas were acknowledged, then bypassed. After one particularly tense exchange, a colleague pulled her aside and said, "You're right, but you need to start reading the room and picking your spots."

Eventually, she adjusted. She chose her words more carefully. She asked fewer questions. She told herself she was being pragmatic. A year later, she admitted that she no longer recognized the leader she had once hoped to be. Nothing dramatic had happened. No scandal. No firing. Just a steady recalibration in response to subtle signals about what was truly rewarded. She later shared that she felt as though she was beginning to lose herself. Her values had not disappeared. She had simply learned, slowly, and subtly, which parts of them were welcome and which carried risk.

C-level executives and senior managers signal to the rest of the organization; often without realizing it, what acceptable conduct, appearance, and behavior should look like. Over time, most organizations reward conformity far more consistently than contribution. What looks like professionalism in adulthood often mirrors what worked on the playground: blend in, stay close to power, and don't disrupt the group. Once hired, many employees quickly learn that fitting in matters more than standing out. In some environments, new hires who try too hard to prove themselves are indirectly discouraged, their initiative interpreted as a critique of the original hiring decision rather than a sign of engagement. The results can border on the absurd. Executives emulate one another's mannerisms, dress, and even grooming. A CEO favors a specific brand of shoe, and soon the leadership team does the same. Another wears baseball caps, polo shirts, and a goatee, and the aesthetic cascades downward. The message is subtle but unmistakable: similarity signals safety.

This pattern extends beyond style. What begins as imitation hardens into selection. Leaders often gravitate toward people who look, speak, and behave as they do. Organizational and social psychologists refer to this as affinity bias. The Center for Talent Innovation found that 71 percent of senior leaders who serve as sponsors, executives who actively advocate for and advance high-potential employees, admit to selecting protégés who share their race and gender, a dynamic that significantly limits advancement opportunities for women and people of color (O'Donnell, 2019). As Shah (2010) describes it, "mini-me syndrome" occurs when executives choose successors who resemble themselves in age, style, experience, and identity. Proximity to power matters. Shared hobbies, shared backgrounds, and informal access, on the golf course or elsewhere, often shape who is seen, trusted, and promoted (O'Donnell, 2019). While a degree of conformity can create clarity and predictability within organizations, unexamined similarity narrows perspective and weakens leadership. What looks like professionalism in adulthood often mirrors what worked on the playground. Standing out on the playground carried with it some risks. Blending in offered protection. Staying close to those who picked teams mattered more than demonstrating ability. Over time, organizations replicate the same logic, rewarding familiarity and compliance over contribution. Awareness of these patterns is not an indictment of individuals; it is a prerequisite for building organizations that reward judgment over likeness and contribution over comfort.

Complicating this further is the language we use to describe leadership itself. Although *servant leadership* remains influential in theory, the word *servant* carries cultural weight. In American society, it is often conflated with servitude rather than service. Some parents from minoritized groups, for example, have discouraged their children from working in the hospitality industry because of its historical association with subjugation. During a training seminar in Turks and Caicos, local participants shared with one of my co-authors that they avoided fishing and farming for similar reasons, linking those practices to colonial exploitation and slavery.

These histories matter. Corporate leadership across sectors remains strikingly homogeneous, often in ways leaders themselves do not consciously recognize. Yet the employees they are charged with leading increasingly come from cultures, identities, and life experiences very different from their own. The question is not whether diversity exists in the workforce; it does, but whether leaders are prepared to recognize, support, and value it.

Research increasingly confirms what many leaders now acknowledge through experience: organizations perform better when they benefit from a range of perspectives rather than a single dominant viewpoint. Teams that draw from varied experiences tend to innovate more effectively and solve problems with greater depth (Roberts & Mayo, 2019). Yet performance gains of this kind do not happen automatically. They depend on leaders who are willing to examine their own blind spots and resist the pull toward sameness that feels efficient, familiar, and safe. This is where many organizations falter. What leaders say they value and what people actually experience day to day often diverge. Formal policies describe ideals; workplace behavior reveals priorities. What employees observe being rewarded or overlooked ultimately defines how the organization really operates. Employees learn quickly which behaviors lead to approval, advancement, or protection, and which invite risk. When there is a gap between stated values and practiced norms, convention wins.

When Culture Overrides Policy

Consider a financial institution that publishes ethical guidelines while tolerating questionable practices. Employees follow what works, not what's written. Culture is not shaped by mission statements; it is shaped by repeated signals. Over time, people adjust their behavior to match what actually leads to approval or advancement. Integrity becomes situational rather than principled. This change is rarely intentional. It is learned, reinforced, and repeated until it feels like common sense. Most people do not arrive at work hoping to compromise their values. Yet even strong moral foundations struggle to withstand environments that reward outcomes at any cost. Ethics training, childhood upbringing, and professional ideals are no match for incentive systems that prioritize profit, speed, and compliance over judgment and responsibility (Craft, 2012). In high-pressure settings, especially those framed as competitive or survival-based, ethical boundaries erode gradually. Individuals who are more susceptible to environmental pressure are pulled along, not because they lack values, but because the culture punishes resistance (Moberg & Caldwell, 2006).

Those who align with dominant norms tend to advance. Among their ranks, we will observe many who fall within the ranks of the Pickers and the Picked. Those who question them often feel marginalized. They become individuals such as the Occasionally Picked and the Benchwarmers, who are seldom chosen for opportunities for growth and advancement within their organizations. Over time, independent thinking gives way to self-preservation. Values alignment becomes less about integrity and more about conformity. People learn which truths are safe to speak, and which are better left unsaid.

Case Studies in Incremental Moral Erosion

The Panama Papers, a massive 2016 leak of confidential documents that exposed how global elites used offshore shell companies to hide wealth and avoid taxes, offer a stark illustration of this phenomenon. At Mossack Fonseca, the law firm at the center of the scandal, leaders defended their actions by insisting they had complied with the technical requirements of the law, even as their practices violated its spirit and intent (Garside & Pegg, 2016; O'Donovan et al., 2019). The firm's principals did not view themselves as unethical. They believed they had done nothing wrong. This is how moral distortion works: repeated rationalization dulls awareness, and self-justification becomes routine. Over time, people come to believe their own explanations.

Closer to home, Wells Fargo's cross-selling scandal followed a similar path. Employees were subjected to relentless pressure to meet unrealistic sales goals in an environment described by former staff as one of fear and intimidation (Ochs, 2016). The creation of millions of fraudulent accounts was not the result of a few rogue actors; it was the predictable outcome of a system that rewarded numbers while ignoring methods (Veetikazhi & Krishnan, 2019). The organization's public language emphasized care and trust. Its internal incentives communicated something else entirely.

At both Mossack Fonseca and Wells Fargo, hiring and promotion practices reinforced the problem. Affinity bias and convention emulation rewarded those who fit existing patterns and complied with expectations. Performance mattered, but fitting in mattered more. Once "the right person" was hired, advancement depended less on contribution and more on alignment with prevailing norms. Ethical education and personal values took a back seat to organizational signals that made clear what was truly rewarded (Craft, 2012).

Incentive systems amplify these patterns. As David Callahan argues in *The Cheating Culture*, rewards shape behavior more powerfully than principles. When success is narrowly defined and aggressively pursued, rule-breaking becomes normalized. The logic spreads: if everyone is doing it, resistance feels naïve rather than noble. Over time, justification replaces judgment, and outcomes eclipse process.

This logic extends beyond corporate life. Athletes use performance-enhancing drugs not because they reject fairness, but because competition is framed as unforgiving. Students use artificial intelligence tools to complete assignments not because they dismiss learning, but because pressure, time constraints, and economic anxiety dominate decision-making. Similarly, the Pickers will often choose colleagues for their teams they feel will help them achieve their goals while forsaking the hidden talent (the Occasionally Picked or Benchwarmers), because they may feel pressured to perform in their workplaces and want people on their team they perceive will help them achieve their goals. Understanding these behaviors does not excuse them; rather, it explains how certain high-pressure environments shape actions.

Callahan's work underscores a critical point: moral erosion is rarely sudden. It unfolds gradually as systems reward shortcuts, celebrate winners without scrutiny, and penalize those who slow the process by asking difficult questions. Incentive systems function like playground rewards. They teach people which behaviors lead to selection, protection, or advancement. Over time, employees stop asking what is right and start asking what works. The lesson is absorbed steadily, reinforced daily, and rarely questioned. As inequality widens and competition intensifies, integrity becomes harder to sustain. Trust erodes. Cynicism grows. And organizations that once prided themselves on excellence begin to settle for compliance.

Failure does not arrive with villains. It arrives with incentives, habits, and unchallenged norms. Recovery, therefore, requires more than insight. It demands courage to interrupt systems that reward the wrong things long enough for distortion to feel normal, and leadership to repeat the playground. This is the underlying danger Chapter 7 confronts as we examine ways to break the cycle promulgated by the Recess Effect.

References

Callahan, D. (2004). *The cheating culture: Why more Americans are doing wrong to get ahead*. Harcourt.

Craft, J. L. (2012). A review of the empirical ethical decision-making literature: 2004–2011. *Journal of Business Ethics*, *117*(2), 221–259.

Garside, J., & Pegg, D. (2016, April 3). The Panama Papers: How the world's rich and famous hide their money offshore. *The Guardian*. https://www.theguardian.com/news/2016/apr/03/the-panama-papers-how-the-worlds-rich-and-famous-hide-their-money-offshore.

Moberg, D. J., & Caldwell, D. F. (2006). An exploratory investigation of the effect of ethical culture in activating moral imagination. *Journal of Business Ethics*, *68*(2), 193–204.

Ochs, J. (2016, September 15). Wells Fargo's toxic sales culture: A lesson in bad leadership. *Business Ethics & Compliance*.

O'Donnell, R. (2019, February 5). How L&D can prevent 'mini-me syndrome' in leadership. HR Dive. Industry Dive. https://www.hrdive.com/news/how-ld-can-prevent-mini-me-syndrome-in-leadership/547492/.

O'Donovan, F., Wagner, H. F., & Zeume, S. (2019). The value of offshore secrets: Evidence from the Panama Papers. *Review of Financial Studies*, *32*(11), 4117–4155.

Roberts, L. M., Mayo, A. J., & Thomas, D. A. (Eds.). (2019). *Race, work, and leadership: New perspectives on the Black experience*. Harvard Business Review Press.

Shah, S. (2010, November 11). Equality: Unconscious bias and the mini-me syndrome. *HR Magazine*. https://www.hrmagazine.co.uk/content/features/equality-unconscious-bias-and-the-mini-me-syndrome.

Veetikazhi, R., & Krishnan, G. (2019). Wells Fargo: Fall from great to miserable: A case study on corporate governance failures. *South Asian Journal of Business and Management Cases*, *8*(1), 88–99.

7

Breaking the Cycle

From Playground to Responsibility

In the previous chapter, we discussed how the things that are deemed unhealthy start to feel acceptable, not through bad intentions, but through repetition. The same behaviors get rewarded, the same shortcuts get excused, and slowly the organization begins to confuse familiarity with competence. What gets reinforced becomes the standard. What gets ignored becomes permission. Recovery begins when leaders stop treating culture as personality and start treating it as intentional design. I did not always understand this. Early in my administrative career, I assumed that modeling strong values would be enough. I eventually learned that systems, not sincerity, determine what endures. This chapter turns toward recovery. When we begin to recognize how early playground experiences still shape how we relate to others, we can start making more conscious choices. That is what lifelong learning looks like in practice.

From Awareness to Design

Recovery does not begin with slogans. It begins with conditions. It begins when leaders recognize that inclusive culture is not what they announce; it is what they consistently reward, protect, and correct. The same "emulate-to-elevate" phenomenon that spreads

DOI: 10.4324/9781003752219-7

conformity can also spread excellence, but only when leadership becomes intentional about what is being replicated.

In other words, if the organization is going to imitate someone, it matters who is worth imitating. During most of our Recess Effect training or classroom sessions, many participants have asked the question: What kind of leadership actually prevents the playground from repeating itself?

Progressive leaders learn to embody the qualities they want others to adopt, not as performance, but as a daily practice (Alexakis, 2011). This goes beyond "setting an example." It is about shaping the environment so that better behavior becomes easier, safer, and more normal than the old habits. My coauthor, George Alexakis, began developing a theory he calls *transcendental leadership,* a concept that parallels servant-leadership. He uses transcendental to describe leaders who bring out peak performance by doing the inner work required to lead cleanly, consistently, and with restraint (Alexakis, 2011).

While transformational leadership can change direction, energy, and performance, transcendental leadership goes further. It reshapes the conditions that influence behavior long after the leader is no longer present. The distinction matters when the goal is not short-term improvement, but lasting cultural repair.

This aligns with the view that strategic leadership operates across levels of self, others, and the organization (Crossan et al., 2008). Like servant-leadership, the credibility of transcendental leadership rests on integrity and a willingness to sacrifice personal ego in service of people and mission, not servitude, but stewardship (Alexakis, 2011). Authentic leadership echoes the same direction. It emphasizes ongoing self-awareness and relationships marked by openness, trust, and genuine regard (Alexakis, 2011). Put plainly: if leaders do the right things in the right way, the system begins to change because the system has new signals to follow.

Transcendental Leadership in Practice

The contrast between progressive leadership and a narrow managerial mindset is sharp. Peter Drucker captured it in a line that still holds: management is doing things right; leadership is doing the right things. Leadership matters because it acts like a catalyst. It influences how people interpret the mission, how they treat one another under pressure, and what they consider permissible when nobody is watching. Savvy leaders stay close to the real obstacles their teams face and continue developing their own practice to remain effective (Drucker, 2009, as cited in US Naval Institute Proceedings, 2016).

The message we give leaders who want to build something enduring is simple: start with yourself. Transcendental leadership may offer one of the clearest pathways for leaders who want to move a culture out of the Recess Effect and into something healthier (Alexakis, 2011; Sanders et al., 2003). While traditional leadership theories often emphasize outward behaviors, positional authority, or outward demonstrations of competence, the transcendental leadership model proposed by Sanders, Hopkins, and Geroy (2003) invites a deeper inquiry, asking not only what effective leaders do, but also what fuels those actions? It also asks what shapes the conditions that make effective leadership possible in the first place? In this view, leadership is not merely a performance or a set of techniques. It is an expression of internal alignment that influences how people relate, interact, and engage with one another over time.

This matters because recovery from the Recess Effect is not achieved by hoping employees "follow the example." Evolved leaders know they cannot command human outcomes. What they can do is cultivate conditions that make the desired outcomes more likely. They begin by transforming themselves, then structuring the environment so that the group dynamics follow.

In organizations, the parallel is straightforward. Recovery accelerates when leaders establish value alignment early and reinforce it consistently. That means hiring, orientation, and training are not treated as administrative steps, but as the moment the culture declares what it truly protects. We cooperate best with people whose core principles do not collide with ours. The "trick," if there is one, is communicating and reinforcing values quickly and clearly. My coauthors and I have witnessed a remarkable change in corporate and nonprofit settings when leaders stop assuming values are understood and start naming them as expectations. The clearer the message, the faster behavior changes.

My own way of communicating values is often through stories, because stories reveal principles without sounding like a lecture. Joseph Campbell's insight still holds:

People forget facts but remember stories (Campbell, 1988). Every leader has a style, but the outcome tends to be consistent. Those who cannot live with the stated values often leave. More importantly, those who remain because their ethics align with the organization's expectations become safer, bolder, and more creative. They stop scanning the room for danger and start contributing. This is where recovery becomes practical: it is not about motivating people as if they are machines. It is about removing what blocks their best instincts.

The most reliable motivation in human beings comes from within. Daniel Pink (2009) popularized what research has long suggested: autonomy, mastery, and purpose are core drivers of sustained motivation. People want room to direct their work, to improve at something meaningful, and to connect effort to purpose. When organizations rely only on external pressure and external rewards, they often get compliance, but they lose ownership. Pink argued that many workplaces use motivation strategies that contradict what science says about performance, especially when the work requires judgment, creativity, or problem-solving (Pink, 2009). Ariely and colleagues found that higher rewards improved performance for simple mechanical tasks, but for cognitive tasks, higher incentives could produce worse outcomes (Ariely et al., 2008).

That research fits the Recess Effect perfectly. When people feel they are being evaluated for *conditional belonging* rather than meaningful contribution, they become cautious. They protect themselves. They imitate the safest signals. They stop taking the risks that innovation requires. Leaders can restore a healthy organizational climate by rebuilding trust and strengthening psychological safety. Recovery, therefore, is not a speech. It is a redesign.

At this point, the path toward recovery comes into focus. The Recess Effect persists not because people lack values or effort, but because systems are designed to reward the wrong instincts. When belonging feels conditional and risk feels unsafe, people adapt by narrowing themselves. They become careful rather than curious. Recovery does not emerge from inspiration alone. It begins when leaders redesign the conditions that shape behavior every day. Leadership changes here, away from pressure and persuasion, and toward cultivation.

Leaders cannot inject motivation into other human beings. Most people begin their careers wanting to do well, to belong, and to feel proud of their contributions. What leaders can do is cultivate that motivation, protect it, and stop crushing it. Expecting people to bring energy into environments that drain it is a contradiction. In practice, leadership is less about fixing personalities and more about shaping conditions. When a flower does not bloom, you adjust the environment, not the flower (Dell'Angelo, 2016).

As such, we will focus on three practical tools leaders can use to cultivate environments where people are motivated to contribute and bring their best to work. The first is intentional investment in training and development. The second is fair and effective compensation. The third is a shared commitment to trust, integrity, and clearly reinforced values.

Leadership Tools for Transformational Change

Wise leaders build interest and ownership through learning and development, not as perks, but as recovery tools. Training and development can help organizations avoid the mini-me trap, create a fairer playing field, and normalize growth opportunities across roles and identities (O'Donnell, 2019). When people gain skills, they gain agency. When they gain agency, they contribute more freely. That is not idealism. That is how healthy cultures regain energy.

And one practical point matters here. Kohn emphasizes that fair pay is not a luxury in a healthy culture; it is foundational.

People cannot bring their best attention to work when compensation anxiety dominates their mental bandwidth (Kohn, 2003). Pink makes a similar point: pay enough to take money off the table (Pink, 2011). Recovery from the Recess Effect requires that leaders remove the distractions that make people feel unsafe, undervalued, or easily replaceable.

So, the path forward is not motivational speeches or another framed poster in the hallway. It is a deliberate reset of what the organization makes easy to practice, what it makes costly to tolerate, and what it refuses to permit. When leaders protect candor, reward sound judgment, and stop confusing urgency with importance, people exhale. They begin to take appropriate risks again. They stop performing for approval and start building for impact. That's what recovery looks like in real time: a workplace where trust becomes practical, not sentimental, and where doing the right thing is supported instead of punished.

Integrity sits at the center of this approach, but not in the simplistic sense of "setting a good example." Evolved leaders understand that people do not change simply because someone above them behaves admirably. They change because the environment around them changes. Transcendental leaders influence outcomes not by issuing directives or modeling behavior in isolation, but by shaping the relational and structural context in which work occurs. They recognize a fundamental truth: human outcomes cannot be commanded. They can only be cultivated. As a result, these leaders begin with themselves, not as a moral exercise, but as a practical one. When leaders alter their own patterns of engagement, decision-making, and interaction, the group dynamic changes with them. This is how change actually happens for the Pickers and the Always Picked in the Recess Effect scenario. We believe this is the foundation for building sustainable connections with colleagues in the workplace.

A simple illustration makes this clear. In a household of four, if one person decides to adopt a fully plant-based diet, the impact rarely stops with that individual. Over time, the entire household begins to eat differently. It happens because daily routines change. Grocery shopping changes. Meals are prepared differently. Cooking two separate dinners becomes inefficient. Without persuasion or pressure, the group adapts. The pattern changes. This is how group dynamics respond to internal transformation. It is also why twelve-step programs, mental health practitioners, and spiritual traditions consistently return to the same premise: meaningful change begins with the self, not as an act of control, but as a catalyst for broader transformation.

Strong leaders extend this understanding into the workplace by intentionally creating motivating environments through values alignment. This does not mean seeking uniformity of personality or background. It means building systems, particularly in hiring, onboarding, training, and development, that clearly communicate what the organization stands for and what it will not compromise. Collaboration works best when people share a core set of values, even while differing in perspective, temperament, and approach. The challenge lies not in declaring values, but in consistently reinforcing them. Over the years, my coauthors and I have witnessed striking organizational shifts when leaders articulate their values clearly and early. The faster values are communicated with consistency, the faster cultures begin to stabilize and evolve.

Leaders communicate values in different ways. Some rely on explicit language and policy; others make priorities visible through everyday decisions. In value-driven environments, the effects are tangible. Psychological safety increases. Candor expands. Creativity rises. Over time, trust deepens.

At the heart of transcendental, servant, and authentic leadership models is a shared recognition: sustained motivation comes from within. External pressure can compel behavior, but it cannot generate commitment. Nobel Peace Prize laureate Muhammad Yunus, founder of the Grameen Bank, has long emphasized that people possess an inherent drive to improve their circumstances when conditions support that impulse. Human beings want agency. That is, they want a sense of control, autonomy, and a meaningful voice in shaping their environment. They want to learn, create, and contribute meaningfully. As Daniel Pink (2011) notes, motivation flourishes when individuals are absorbed in the work itself rather than preoccupied with external rewards such as grades, money, or status.

These ideas entered the mainstream through Daniel Pink's widely viewed TED Talk (https://www.ted.com/talks/dan_pink_the_puzzle_of_motivation), which exposed the gap between what decades of research tell us about motivation and what many organizations still practice (Pink, 2009). Subsequent research has confirmed that incentive-heavy systems weaken performance when work requires judgment, creativity, or problem-solving (Ariely et al., 2008).

This is where recovery from the Recess Effect becomes tangible. Guiding and facilitating, rather than relying on carrots and sticks, strengthens the intrinsic motivation already present in people. Alfie Kohn's extensive research underscores this point. When organizations rely too heavily on external rewards, they inadvertently weaken interest in the work itself. Creativity declines. Engagement drops. Satisfaction erodes. Kohn argues that environments fostering autonomy, meaningful work, and growth opportunities produce deeper commitment and higher-quality outcomes (Kohn, 2019).

What ultimately sustains recovery is not motivation itself, but the environment that either protects or erodes it over time. When people experience consistency between stated values and lived expectations, effort stabilizes. When good judgment is rewarded rather than punished, people stop performing and start contributing. This is the daily work of leadership: making it easier to do the right thing than to survive by imitation.

Regardless of industry, the most valuable resource in any organization is not its buildings, its brand and reputation, nor its technology, but the people who log off their computers at the end of the day and head home. They carry the culture with them. They return with it the next morning. These individuals, not brick and mortar, are the beating heart of any organization, and they contribute to its reputation.

This orientation naturally leads to customer-centered leadership. Those closest to customers, such as cashiers, servers, security staff, and frontline professionals, carry the organization's reputation daily. Leaders who understand this protect and empower those roles. Support, autonomy, rest, and development are not perks; they are investments. Research from Gallup and

Harvard Business Review consistently links employee engagement to customer loyalty, retention, and performance. Caring for employees strengthens the entire system.

Leadership grounded in empathy, reflection, and awareness offers a credible path forward. It does not require heroic personalities, but disciplined cultivation of environments where motivation, judgment, and integrity are protected.

Transcendental leadership reframes the leader's role. Not as commander. Not as a performer. But as the architect of conditions. When leaders accept that responsibility, the emulation-to-elevation phenomenon becomes possible. Culture begins to heal. And the patterns learned on the playground finally lose their grip.

By the time organizations acknowledge the need for recovery, leadership is often reduced to style or tone. That lens misses the point. Recovery is not achieved by adopting a kinder tone or more thoughtful language. It depends on whether leaders disrupt the conditions that allow harm to take hold and persist. Some approaches end up recreating the very dynamics that caused damage. Others impose stability without addressing what lies beneath. Only a small number engage the systems and norms that determine whether recovery holds.

Figure 7.1 illustrates leadership not as a set of interchangeable styles, but as a progression of responsibility and cultural impact over time. Moving upward means moving from control to cultivation, and from managing visible behavior to reshaping the underlying conditions that govern belonging, power, and contribution. While inspirational and care-centered leadership can generate momentum and relief, recovery becomes durable only when leaders regulate themselves, redesign systems, and set boundaries that prevent the reemergence of playground dynamics. The figure clarifies why recovery fails when leadership stops at intention, and why it succeeds when culture, not charisma, becomes the work. Thus, at the Transcendental Leadership level, the Apple Effect is actively cultivated.

What distinguishes these approaches is not intent, but endurance. Many leadership styles can generate movement. Far fewer prevent regression. When systems reward good judgment instead

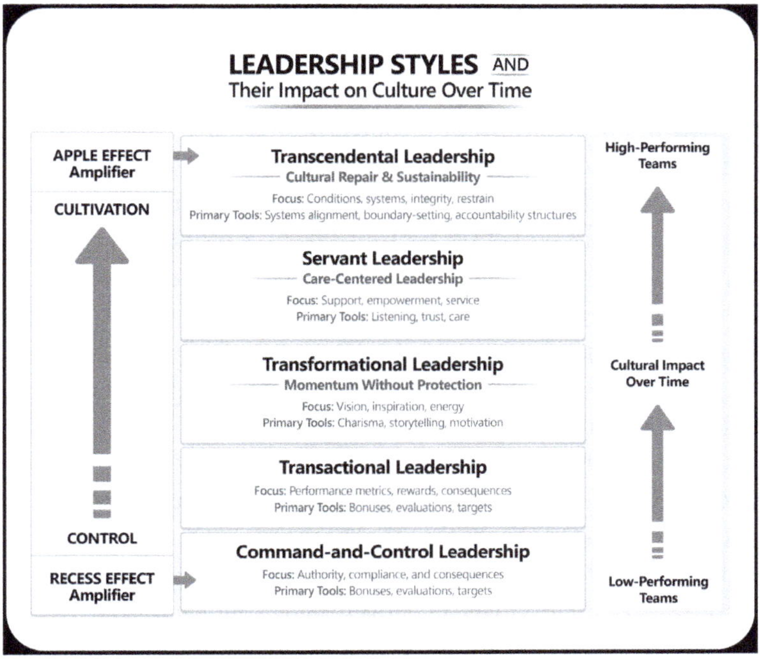

FIGURE 7.1 Leadership Styles and Their Impact on Culture

of sameness, and integrity instead of visibility, the playground loses its grip. Culture begins to self-correct, even when leaders step back. That is the difference between clear improvements rather than superficial repairs to cultures negatively impacted by the Recess Effect.

Some researchers who study leadership tell us that team creativity and innovation will be catalyzed when leaders within organizations apply the right leadership style (Peng et al., 2019). Positive leadership can increase staff's motivation, self-efficacy, and satisfaction (Men et al., 2018; Lin et al., 2020), while negative leadership leads to uncertainty, negative emotions, and low performance in team activities (Peng et al., 2019).

Notable leadership scholar John Kotter has observed that continuity among personnel tends to produce a strong and enduring organizational culture. For example, when leadership is composed largely of individuals who share similar backgrounds, values, and assumptions, a high-context culture often develops, characterized by shared norms and implicit expectations, where much of what matters is understood rather than explicitly stated. However, when new leaders enter the organization from different cultural or professional backgrounds, they may introduce perspectives and values that differ from those of the dominant group. These differences can alter norms around tolerance, decision-making, and communication, and, if not intentionally managed, may create tension or conflict within the leadership team.

In some organizations, leadership forms a community that mirrors the Picked and Always Picked, cohesive but not inclusive. The Apple Effect calls leaders to build unity that does not depend on sameness.

For organizational leaders to truly practice service-minded and transcendental leadership, they must envision themselves as operating as a servant-leader. George Manners argued that "servant leaders create situations where the organization can learn to manage itself so that it ensures its growth and sustainability" (Manner, 2025). Employees require much from their leaders today, particularly credibility. The process of building community within an organization by its management can begin by changing the group dynamics, rearranging the organizational structure, and setting an example for employees as well as stakeholders. Building an impressive, innovative, and enduring company is not a matter of talent versus control systems but requires leaders who know how to recruit, inspire, retain, develop, and lead talented and ethical people so that their actions and their interactions have profound influences on their organizations (Maccoby, 2002).

Professional Decorum as Cultural Signal

Professionalism requires the application of skills learned at an occupational level. However, professional decorum—the essence of professionalism—means implementing the conventions of cultured behavior and mannerisms. I have noted in one of my previously published articles that a polite tone of voice, patience, a positive attitude, and most of all, *a willingness to facilitate the needs of others* demonstrate professional decorum (Rice & Rice, 2008).

Professionalism extends to composing virtual communication messages using generally accepted online etiquette. A professional attitude amounts to a great asset when it is genuinely practiced, and it can create an organizational culture of mutual respect. Mutual respect represents the cornerstone of necessary organizational shifts toward a highly valued workplace among those who work there (R. Green, Jr., personal communications, February 21, 2024). A well-known and often-cited study linked specific leadership styles with employee stress and emotional well-being (Walumbwa et al., 2008).

The Recess Effect's Impact on Customer Service

When leaders fail to heed the lessons of the *Recess Effect* within their internal team-building processes, the same exclusionary behaviors experienced by the Occasionally Picked and the Benchwarmers can spill over into how the organization engages its customers. In such cases, customers may receive treatment akin to that afforded to Occasionally Picked or the Benchwarmers, rather than being fully valued and included. This dynamic can be observed in the way some major retail organizations approach and interact with their customers.

Some retail stores become so large that the management seems to forget that the business they receive from their customers is the quintessential factor that keeps them in business. I stated earlier that increasing the size of an organization negatively changes the way it treats customers (along with products and workers). How often have customers stood in line for hours for a particular service or even to pay a bill, only to be shown little patience or respect once they have reached the *customer* service representative? How often do customers experience long waits at a counter before the receptionist acknowledges their presence? Some customers leave stores having bought nothing because of poor customer service relations.

The same holds true for many medical institutions and doctor's offices, where people more often feel like cattle than high-paying customers. People in organizations, particularly large ones, seem to forget that the organization would not exist if it were not for the customer, client, patient, etc. Instead of treating people like paying customers who expect genuine care and patience, the management and staff at some of these places all but say, "This would be a really great place to work if it wasn't for all these pesky customers!" So, in truth, customers, clients, or patients in this scenario have now become Benchwarmers.

As documented previously in this text, the problem begins with managers incentivized to meet the bottom line rather than to service people's needs and wants. In countless cases, financially incentivized managers focus on getting the customer to pay more instead of satisfying that customer. They call it "upselling." They encourage salespeople to pursue extra sales that do not serve the customer's best interest. If the educators and managers do not exhibit the proper example of a transcendent, authentic servant-leadership within their own organizations, how do future employees and professionals act accordingly? Many people learn best by observation. The phrase, "You've got to walk the walk, not just talk the talk," conjures a clarion call from individuals leery of hearing more insincere and overplayed smooth words from people in positions of authority.

Key Takeaways on Recovery through Transcendental Leadership

People now expect to see words transformed into action! Servant leaders who demonstrate genuine care for their employees command respect. They seek to meet organizational associates where they stand in their experience and understanding of their work, that is, whether they are seen as the Pickers, the Picked or the Benchwarmers. They use these individual starting points to help associates strengthen their skills as they face workplace challenges. In turn, this process encourages employees to do the same—not only for the management who largely determine their financial fates and workplace environment but also for the customers who will ultimately benefit.

Recovery from the Recess Effect does not require heroic leaders (i.e. Pickers) or perfect systems. It requires leaders willing to accept a less visible, more demanding responsibility: shaping the conditions that determine how people behave when no one is watching. Culture does not change because of what leaders say in moments of inspiration. It changes because of what they make easier, what they make harder, and what they refuse to excuse. When leaders protect judgment, reward integrity, and interrupt patterns that favor familiarity over contribution, the need for constant enforcement diminishes. People begin to regulate themselves. The organization starts to breathe differently.

This is where transcendental leadership matters. Not as a label, but as a posture. Leaders who approach their role as architects rather than performers understand that influence outlasts presence only when systems are aligned with values. They begin with themselves, not simply to model virtue, but to remove distortion. As their own patterns of engagement, decision-making, and restraint shift, the group follows. Not because it was told to, but because the environment has changed. The Apple Effect becomes visible here, not as a metaphor, but as a lived experience. What once felt risky becomes safe. What once required courage becomes normal.

Recovery holds only when these conditions are reinforced beyond individual leaders. Even the most thoughtful leadership will see old patterns return if structures remain unchanged. Culture stabilizes when recovery is translated into everyday practices: how teams are built, how decisions are made, how conflict is handled, how accountability works, and how belonging is reinforced without conformity. The next chapter turns to this work, examining how organizations move from cultural intention to operational integrity, and how recovery becomes durable rather than dependent on who happens to be in charge.

References

Alexakis, G. (2011). Transcendental leadership: Building environments where integrity shapes performance. *Journal of Business & Economics Research (JBER)*, *9*(9), 47–52.

Ariely, D., Gneezy, U., Loewenstein, G., & Mazar, N. (2008). Large stakes and big mistakes. *Review of Economic Studies, 76*(2), 451–469. https://doi.org/10.1111/j.1467-937X.2008.00534.x.

Campbell, J. (1988). *The power of myth*. Doubleday.

Crossan, M., Dusya, V., & Nanji, A. (2008). Transcendent leadership: Strategic leadership in dynamic environments. *The Leadership Quarterly, 19*(5), 569–581.

Dell'Angelo, T. (2016). When a flower doesn't bloom, you fix the environment in which it grows, not the flower. *Journal of Invitational Theory and Practice, 22*, 1–3.

Drucker, P. F. (2009). *Management challenges for the 21st century*. HarperBusiness.

Kohn, A. (2003). *Punished by rewards: The trouble with gold stars, incentive plans, A's, praise, and other bribes*. Houghton Mifflin.

Kohn, A. (2019). *The myth of the spoiled child: Challenging the conventional wisdom about children and parenting*. Da Capo Press.

Lin, C.-P., Xian, J., Li, B., & Huang, H. (2020). Transformational leadership and employee creativity: The mediating role of psychological safety. *Journal of Business Research, 109*, 84–94.

Maccoby, M. (2002). The productive narcissist: The promise and peril of visionary leadership. *Harvard Business Review*, 80(1), 92–101.

Manner, G. (2025). Servant leadership and sustainable organizational growth. *Leadership Today Review*.

Men, L. R., Qin, Y. S., & Jin, J. (2018). Fostering employee trust via authentic leadership: The mediating role of transparent communication. *Public Relations Review, 44*(3), 343–352.

O'Donnell, C. P., & Center for Talent Innovation. (2019). *The sponsor dividend: Reaping the rewards of high-stakes advocacy*. Center for Talent Innovation.

Peng, J., Li, M., Wang, Z., & Lin, Y. (2019). Transformational leadership and team innovation: The mediating role of team climate. *Journal of Leadership & Organizational Studies, 26*(4), 412–425.

Pink, D. H. (2009). *Drive: The surprising truth about what motivates us*. Riverhead Books.

Pink, D. H. (2011). The puzzle of motivation [Video]. TED Conferences. https://www.ted.com/talks/dan_pink_the_puzzle_of_motivation.

Rice, L. A., & Rice, C. M. (2008). Professional decorum in leadership communication. *Journal of Organizational Culture and Communication, 12*(2), 45–58.

Sanders, J. E., Hopkins, W. E., & Geroy, G. D. (2003). From transactional to transcendental: Toward an integrated theory of leadership. *Journal of Leadership Studies, 10*(4), 21–31.

Walumbwa, F. O., Avolio, B. J., Gardner, W. L., Wernsing, T. S., & Peterson, S. J. (2008). Authentic leadership: Development and validation of a theory-based measure. *Journal of Management, 34*(1), 89–126.

8

Outgrowing the Playground

Choosing Who You Become

The Developmental Roots of the Recess Effect

The Recess Effect originates in early relationship development, long before individuals enter classrooms, workplaces, or organizations. In childhood, relationships are defined first by *dependence*. Infants rely entirely on caregivers for survival, regulation, and meaning. Parents serve as the primary point of reference, influencing how safety, trust, and attention are experienced. As children grow, this dependency expands beyond the family to include teachers, caregivers, and peers. Children come to expect consistency, inclusion, and continuity in these secondary relationships, even though those environments are often less stable and less attentive than the home.

During the early school years, children begin forming peer attachments that are intense but fragile. I remember watching a first grader dissolve into tears when her "best friend" chose to sit next to someone else at lunch. Nothing dramatic had happened. No argument. Just a change in proximity. Yet the emotional weight was enormous. Friendships change quickly. Inclusion and exclusion carry emotional weight. Children expect relationships to endure in the same way parental relationships do, and

DOI: 10.4324/9781003752219-8

when they do not, disappointment and anxiety emerge. These early experiences introduce the first seeds of the Recess Effect: learning who belongs, who holds power, and how social standing can change without warning. At this stage, children are not consciously cultivating relationships; they are reacting to them. Belonging feels conditional, and social cues become signals for safety.

From Dependence to Interdependence

As children mature into adolescence and young adulthood, relationships move toward *interdependence*. Parents gradually encourage autonomy while remaining central figures. Teachers transform from being sole authorities to facilitators of learning. Peers become increasingly influential as individuals test identity, values, and social standing. This stage lays the groundwork for how people relate to authority and groups later in life.

It is also the stage where the Recess Effect becomes most visible. Social norms intensify. Group hierarchies solidify. Approval, visibility, and alignment with influential figures take on greater importance. Individuals learn, often unconsciously, how to read power dynamics, adapt behavior, and protect their position within the group. In high school, this can look like a student laughing at a joke they do not find funny simply because the most influential person in the room told it. The skills developed here are not inherently negative. They become problematic when they remain unexamined and unrefined into adulthood.

Independence and the Illusion of Maturity

Adulthood is often framed as a stage of *independence*, but independence is frequently misunderstood. While adults gain autonomy from parental and educational authority, the relational patterns formed earlier do not disappear. The focal point moves toward the self, yet many individuals carry unresolved expectations about approval, security, and belonging into their professional lives.

In the workplace, this often appears as a return to interdependence driven by performance and evaluation. Employees learn quickly which behaviors are rewarded, which opinions are safe, and which risks threaten standing. I have watched talented professionals soften their language mid-sentence when they sensed a senior executive's impatience, recalibrating in real time to protect their standing. Performance reviews, promotions, and incentives can reinforce early lessons: fit in, stay visible, and avoid missteps. What looks like collaboration on the surface may be driven internally by self-protection and advancement rather than shared purpose.

As Peter Drucker (2009) cautioned, incentive systems can systematically distort judgment. When success is measured narrowly, individuals stop asking whether decisions are right and begin asking whether they will be rewarded. The Recess Effect resurfaces here not because people lack ethics, but because systems reward familiar survival strategies learned long ago.

The Apple Effect: Cultivating Relational Maturity

The Apple Effect represents a shift beyond these inherited patterns. Where the Recess Effect reflects stalled relational development, the Apple Effect reflects *relational maturity*. It begins when individuals take responsibility for how they relate to power, authority, and others, regardless of context. Rather than seeking belonging through imitation or self-promotion, individuals ground their relationships in trust, honesty, and respect.

This shift is not automatic. It requires conscious adjustment. Early socialization exerts a persistent pull, and the Recess Effect does not disappear without effort. Mentors, role models, and leaders play a critical role in interrupting old scripts by modeling healthier relational norms. Over time, service to others replaces self-protection as the organizing principle of interaction.

Growing beyond the playground does not mean rejecting ambition or achievement. It means no longer letting early survival strategies dictate adult behavior. When individuals reach this stage, relationships stabilize. Integrity replaces performance. Contribution matters more than optics. And the conditions are created for healthier systems to take root.

The Apple Effect begins in the home because family is where early relationship habits are first rehearsed: how we listen, how we repair, how we share power, and how we treat people when we are tired, irritated, or disappointed. Parents can teach children to be participatory in everyday interactions by modeling respect, accountability, and consideration. But the Apple Effect does not stay in the home. In modern life, schools often carry an even heavier load in shaping social behavior simply because of time and exposure. Many adults spend 35–45 hours a week at work. If parents leave at 8:30 a.m. and return after 5:00 p.m., the window for family connection on a typical weekday is narrow. Children, likewise, spend most of their waking hours in a school ecosystem with teachers, aides, classmates, coaches, school administrators, counselors, and aftercare staff. For better or worse, schools function as a second home, and for many children, they become the primary laboratory for belonging, conflict, and identity.

That reality matters because the Recess Effect is not only learned at recess. It is reinforced in systems where adults are stretched thin and where children are left to invent social rules in the absence of consistent guidance. Moving away from the Recess Effect, therefore, cannot be treated as a vague hope that people will "do better." It requires an Apple Effect approach to personal responsibility and relational practice. Throughout this book, we have avoided using the word "change" to describe what individuals must do. The better word to describe the transformation required might be *adjustment*. Nick Bollettieri, one of the most successful tennis coaches in history, emphasized that elite performance grows through adjustment, not shaming people with the demand to "change."

The same principle applies here. People do not undo years of learned social coping overnight. They make repeated, conscious adjustments: in how they respond, how they interpret others, how they handle conflict, and how they decide what kind of colleague, teammate, or leader they intend to be.

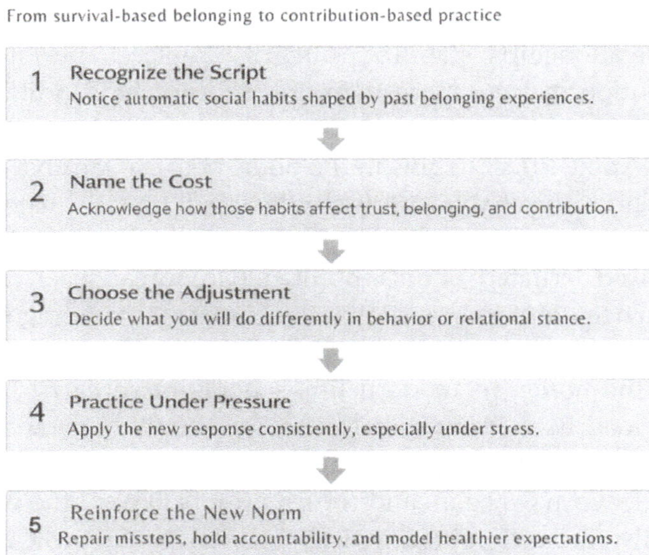

FIGURE 8.1 Five-step Apple Effect Framework

The Apple Effect is a unitary process because it begins inside the individual and then comes through in relationships. It moves from insight to practice, from intention to pattern. The pace of improvement depends on willingness and repetition, but the direction is open to anyone who decides that memories of how they and their schoolmates behaved on the playground will not serve as their only blueprint. For that reason, we propose a five-step process for personalizing the Apple Effect, a practical pathway for moving from inherited relational habits to intentional ones (see Figure 8.1). We will return to each step in later chapters. For now, the point is simple: recovery is not abstract. It becomes real when people commit to adjustments they can repeat under pressure.

Recognizing the Script

William Ury proposed that a way to look outside of oneself when faced with conflict with others was a practice known as "going to the balcony" (Ury, 1991). It is a process by which individuals can examine conflicts or difficult situations by almost stepping out of themselves, both emotionally and mentally, in order to gain a new perspective on the situation with which they are faced.

In the case of the Recess Effect, the Pickers and the Picked might consider what it would feel like if they were left out of projects or activities that could allow them to network among their colleagues or that might turn into opportunities for upward mobility in their organizations. What could it mean for their sense of self-esteem and for their careers? If this empathetic exercise is done with care, it may result in a change in behavior when teams are being selected for future projects or activities in the workplace (Rice & Rice, 2008, 2012).

Benchwarmers may consider advocating for themselves by discussing their concerns with team leaders in one-to-one meetings. It is usually best to avoid public admonition of team leaders, as this tactic may backfire and may cause more conflict. Concurrently, Benchwarmers may choose to confer with allies, within their departments and teams or with mentors, trusted colleagues, or allies that sit elsewhere in the organization. Mentors within the workplace are colleagues who are not directly involved with the departments where Benchwarmers spend most of their time and may be able to provide objective yet potent insights into how to approach situations where Benchwarmers feel overlooked. These allies can also help advocate for the Benchwarmers behind the scenes to redress oversight in team selection or relating to opportunities for growth.

Growing beyond the playground is not a rejection of where we came from. It is an acknowledgment of it. The Recess Effect shaped many of us before we had language, power, or choice to truly understand what was going on. What matters now is not whether those patterns exist, but whether we continue to let them operate unchecked. The Apple Effect offers a different path, one grounded in awareness, restraint, and deliberate practice. It asks individuals to stop outsourcing responsibility for their behavior to systems, titles, or incentives, and to recognize their role in shaping the relational climate around them.

Name the Cost

This work is neither quick nor comfortable. Adjustment requires attention, repetition, and the willingness to notice one's actions when under pressure. Old scripts resurface most reliably when stakes are high, time is short, or approval feels uncertain. That might mean cutting someone off in a meeting because you fear losing control of the narrative. Or staying silent when you see a colleague sidelined because you do not want to be next. That is precisely why personalizing the Apple Effect matters. When individuals commit to practicing healthier relational patterns consistently, they reduce their reliance on early survival strategies. Over time, belonging becomes less conditional, contribution becomes more authentic, and trust becomes easier to sustain. What begins as a personal shift gradually strengthens teams, cultures, and institutions.

The Recess Effect thrives in ambiguity. The Apple Effect takes hold through clarity and practice. As the next section will explore, recovery deepens when personal responsibility is reinforced by structures that support it. When individuals and systems align, cultural repair stops depending on personality or position and becomes part of how work actually gets done. Growing beyond the playground is not the end of the journey. It is the point where personal responsibility for all parties within the Recess Effect cycle becomes real, and where the conditions for lasting change finally come into focus.

Choose the Adjustment

A key adjustment is building awareness of the patterns of exclusion promulgated by the Recess Effect. Communication and conflict resolution strategies form the next step in this awareness building wherein each member of the team recognizes where they are in the teambuilding process and chooses to exercise some agency in addressing instances when individuals feel left out. Active listening becomes critical as each person involved in team building processes listens attentively to others' viewpoints in the route to finding solutions, where new team members are recruited, and strategies are in place to bring them up to speed on projects, if they don't yet have the requisite skills. Together through collaborative problem solving, they can tackle challenges and make up for gaps in knowledge or skill. This agency allows individuals to move beyond denial of fault when mistakes are made, shifting blame or self-pitying toward taking action to enhance team building, capacity, and consequently, completing whatever task is set before them (Rice & Rice, 2008, 2012).

Team leaders (the Pickers) can become roving mediators to assist in conflict management within their teams and encourage collaboration among all team members. They can set ground rules for respectful communication to ensure psychological safety for everyone. The Pickers can take ownership of effective conflict management when mistakes are made or when there are disagreements between themselves, the Picked, and those who were formerly Benchwarmers. Finally, through training and development, everyone on the team can be encouraged to coach or mentor less-skilled members to ensure that they get the job done (Rice & Rice, 2012).

Practice Under Pressure: Outgrowing the Playground

Choosing beyond the playground is not about erasing history or rejecting ambition. It is about refusing to let outdated survival strategies govern present responsibility. Once leaders see how early social habits influence decision-making, neutrality disappears. Continuing to react from familiar roles becomes a choice, not an accident.

Leadership maturity shows up under pressure. It appears in how feedback is delivered, how disagreement is handled, how visibility is distributed, and how power is exercised when belonging feels uncertain. In these moments, leaders either repeat the dynamics of the playground or interrupt them. There is no passive option.

The Recess Effect loses its grip not through insight alone, but through repeated, intentional adjustment. Each choice of psychological safety over prioritizing judgmental preconceptions, contribution over conformity, and responsibility over reflex weakens its influence. Over time, these choices reshape culture. They signal what is safe, what is valued, and what will no longer be rewarded.

Choosing beyond the playground antics is where leadership becomes visible, but it is not where the work ends. Individual choice must eventually be reinforced by collective norms, shared expectations, and systems that sustain better behavior over time. The next chapter turns to how organizations translate individual leadership choices into cultural practices, so progress moves to structural organizational practices that do not solely depend on personality, courage, or constant vigilance.

Reinforce the New Norm: Choosing Who You Become

The Recess Effect persists not because people are broken, but because many continue to rely on social strategies learned in childhood. These strategies helped children survive loosely supervised peer systems, like on the playground or during activities. They offered ways to avoid exclusion, secure approval, or reduce risk when adults were absent or inconsistent. In that context, they worked for some children but not for others.

The problem is not that these strategies existed. The problem is that they were rarely examined, guided, or interrupted, and many adults continue to use them long after the context has changed. In early childhood, adults actively structured social behavior. Kindergarten classrooms were high-touch environments where norms like sharing, waiting one's turn, and including others were explicitly taught and reinforced. But as children moved into the early elementary years, that guidance slowly receded. Peer systems were left to regulate themselves.

What had once been protected by adult presence became negotiated through survival. Children adapted. Strategies formed. Patterns of conformity, self-promotion, withdrawal, or control emerged not as immaturity, but as practical responses to unstructured social risk. Those patterns did not disappear. They matured.

This chapter marks a change in responsibility. Once leaders understand how early social strategies shape adult behavior, insight is no longer enough. Leadership begins at the point where awareness turns into choice. This chapter is not about repairing the past or assigning blame. It is about recognizing when familiar responses no longer serve the work, the people, or the mission, and choosing differently, especially under pressure.

Choosing beyond the playground requires more than good intentions. It requires discipline. It requires noticing when inherited habits are driving decisions about authority, belonging, visibility, and risk. Most importantly, it requires accepting that leadership is revealed not in moments of comfort, but in moments when old survival strategies feel easiest to reach for.

In our professional culture, leadership strength is often misread. Traits such as humility, empathy, restraint, and self-awareness are frequently discounted, while dominance, certainty, and visibility are mistaken for competence. These preferences are not accidental. They mirror the same social rewards learned early in life, where being noticed, chosen, or feared often carried more value than being thoughtful or fair.

The Recess Effect reinforces these distortions over time. Behaviors that once helped children navigate unsupervised social environments resurface in adult settings as leadership habits. Withdrawal becomes silence in meetings. Self-promotion becomes performative confidence. Control becomes rigidity, resistant to challenge or change. None of these behaviors are inherently malicious. They are adaptive strategies carried forward without recalibration.

Leadership development begins when individuals recognize that what once protected them may now constrain them. The goal is not to suppress instinct, but to examine it. Under pressure, most people default to familiar roles learned early. Pickers assert control. The Picked seek approval or visibility. Benchwarmers retreat or disengage. These are not fixed identities. They are conditioned responses.

The work of leadership is learning to pause at the moment of default and choose differently. I have had to make that pause myself more than once. That choice matters most when the stakes are high, feedback is ambiguous, and belonging feels uncertain. In those moments, leaders either reenact the dynamics of the playground or interrupt them. Character shapes what someone is capable of. Conditioning shapes what they do first. Leadership is the choice that follows.

At that point, explanation gives way to responsibility. Understanding how patterns formed may offer clarity, but leadership is revealed in whether those patterns are allowed to continue. What matters is not the framework itself, but the discipline of choice. Leaders notice inherited habits, interrupt default responses, and choose intentionally when pressure is highest.

These choices are not made once. They are practiced repeatedly, especially in moments when familiar habits feel efficient, justified, or safe. Leadership maturity begins with awareness. Leaders must first recognize how early social environments shaped their instincts around approval, visibility, conflict, and authority. What feels natural under pressure is rarely neutral. It is usually learned. Awareness alone, however, is insufficient. The work requires interruption. Leaders must learn to pause when automatic responses surface, especially those that prioritize conformity, control, or self-protection over judgment and responsibility.

The final step is intentional action under pressure. This is where leadership becomes visible. Choosing responses aligned with values that prioritize inclusion and fairness, substantive contribution, and long-term impact often carries a cost. It may risk approval, comfort, or status in the moment, but it is also often the choice worth making.

References

Drucker, P. F. (2009). *Management challenges for the 21st century*. Harper Business.

Rice, C. M., & Rice, L. A. (2012). Avoiding the Recess Effect: The dynamics of inclusion and exclusion in conflict resolution training in community organizations. In C. L. Duckworth & C. D. Kelley (Eds.), *Conflict resolution and the scholarship of engagement: Partnerships transforming conflict*. Cambridge Scholars Publishing.

Rice, L. A., & Rice, C. M. (2008). The role of conflict management in human resource development in the hospitality industry. In D. V. Tesone (Ed.), *Handbook of hospitality and tourism human resource management*. Elsevier.

Ury, W. (1991). *Getting past no: Negotiating in difficult situations*. Bantam Books.

9

Designing Cultures That Don't Recreate the Playground

Up to this point, this book has focused on how early social environments shape behavior, and how leaders learn to interrupt those patterns when they surface under pressure. We have examined how the Recess Effect persists through habit, reward, and silence, and how leadership begins when awareness turns into choice.

By the time leaders reach the point of choosing differently under pressure, they have already done difficult work. They have examined their defaults. They have learned to interrupt inherited social strategies. They have accepted responsibility for how they present themselves when belonging feels uncertain. But individual leadership maturity, on its own, is not enough. Emerging research confirms that when organizational cultures emphasize collaboration and shared values, leaders are more likely to adopt constructive leadership behaviors that support psychological well-being and sustained performance. Conversely, cultures that lack supportive norms tend to produce less adaptive leadership dynamics (Kuncoro & Thaha, 2023).

Culture always wins over character when character stands alone. Organizations do not fail because people lack values. They fail because systems incrementally reward behaviors that contradict those values. What feels like a leadership problem is often a

DOI: 10.4324/9781003752219-9

design problem. The Recess Effect persists not because individuals keep choosing poorly, but because environments continue to normalize, reward, and protect the very dynamics people are trying to outgrow.

I once worked with a leadership team that sincerely believed they valued and encouraged collaboration. Yet their bonus structure rewarded only individual performance metrics. No one was trying to undermine teamwork. The system simply told the truth about what mattered most. When structure honors individuals but not teams, collaboration becomes aspirational rather than operational.

This chapter turns from personal leadership choice to collective responsibility. It examines how organizations, schools, and institutions either reinforce early playground dynamics or deliberately disrupt them. The question is no longer, *How do I lead differently?* The question becomes, *What does this environment make normal, rewarded, and repeatable?*

Unsupervised playgrounds taught children powerful lessons. Visibility mattered. Being chosen mattered. Avoiding embarrassment mattered. When adult guidance faded after the early grades, children were left to organize social life on their own. Hierarchies formed quickly. Power went unchecked. Exclusion became instructional. I remember watching a recess where the same three children decided every game. The teacher stood nearby, scanning for physical conflict, unaware that social rules were being written in plain sight.

When performance is measured narrowly, people compete for visibility rather than focus on substantive contributions. When leaders are promoted for confidence rather than competence, dominance is mistaken for capability. When feedback is inconsistent or political, people learn to stay quiet, nod along even when they disagree, or side with whoever holds the most power.

This is why leadership courage alone is unsustainable. Asking individuals to "do the right thing" inside cultures that reward the opposite eventually produces fatigue, withdrawal, or conformity. Over time, people stop choosing. They adapt. The Recess Effect becomes embedded not through cruelty, but through repetition.

In one organization I observed, airtime during meetings gradually became a currency of influence. Some colleagues spoke over others or interrupted mid-sentence to secure visibility. The loudest voices were perceived as the most competent. Thoughtful contributors began shortening their remarks or withdrawing entirely.

Designing cultures that do not recreate the playground requires intentional structure. It means deciding, explicitly, what behaviors will be reinforced, and which will no longer be protected. Across the employee life cycle, this includes shaping hiring, evaluation, promotion, and accountability practices to reward substance over appearance, thoughtful decision-making over loud confidence, and doing what's right even if it risks popularity or comfort.

This can be as practical as rotating who leads meetings, publishing transparent promotion criteria, or evaluating managers on how well they develop others rather than how visible they are to senior leadership. When growth and development become measurable expectations, not informal favors, culture begins to change.

One structural investment that strengthens this shift is formal coaching training for supervisors and leaders. Coaching equips leaders to ask better questions, provide developmental feedback, and cultivate autonomy rather than dependence. Research suggests that organizations that embed coaching practices into leadership development see measurable gains in engagement and performance (Peláez Zuberbühler et al., 2020). In other words, development becomes a system, not a slogan.

Importantly, this work does not belong only to executives. Teachers, principals, school administrators, managers, and team leads all function as culture designers. Wherever adults set norms, enforce boundaries, or allow behavior to pass unchallenged, they are teaching. The question is whether they are reinforcing kindergarten lessons about fairness, patience, and shared responsibility, or abandoning them in favor of hierarchy and survival.

In kindergarten, adults are highly present. Expectations are explicit. Children are taught to take turns, repair harm, include others, and wait for their moment. Power is moderated. Behavior is guided. Belonging is protected. Somewhere between first and third grade, that model fades. As supervision decreases, adults often step back, assuming children will "figure it out." What they actually figure out is how to wield power. The same pattern repeats in organizations. Early-career employees receive structure and support. As stakes rise, guidance recedes. Adults as employees are left to navigate politics without guardrails, and the playground over time returns.

The Apple Effect offers a different approach. It assumes that maturity does not eliminate the need for structure. It recognizes that ethical behavior must be reinforced, not merely encouraged. Cultures that sustain healthy leadership do not rely on heroics. They rely on design. When environments consistently reinforce fairness, accountability, and contribution, individuals no longer need exceptional courage to act well. The system does the heavy lifting.

Designing cultures that do not recreate the playground is not about control. It is about clarity. It is about making expectations visible, consequences predictable, and values operational. When people know what is rewarded, they adapt accordingly. The question is whether adaptation leads toward maturity or regression.

The Apple Effect becomes durable only when individual leadership choices are reinforced by collective norms. When leaders choose judgment over reflex and systems support that choice, culture shifts. Over time, what once required effort becomes expectation. What once felt risky becomes routine. This is how organizations move beyond survival and toward substantive contribution. And this is also how leadership stops depending solely on the cult of personality of just a handful of individuals within an organization. Contemporary leadership research highlights the need for leaders to master a wider range of behaviors that align with organizational transformation efforts, suggesting that leadership cannot be cultivated in isolation from the systems that reinforce it (Harvard Business Publishing, 2024).

Up to this point, we have examined how early social systems shape behavior, how leaders can interrupt inherited patterns, and how organizations either reinforce or dismantle those dynamics. The final question remains: *What does this look like in practice?*

Research also shows that leadership behavior profoundly influences organizational norms, trust, and psychological safety, which in turn shape culture, engagement, and innovation (Addai et al., 2023). Ultimately, however, organizational culture, not charisma, determines whether enlightened leadership endures. I have seen charismatic leaders ignite organizations for a season, only to watch the culture revert once they left. Strong leaders can spark change. Only strong systems make it last. Systems are the structures that govern daily decisions: how people are hired, evaluated, promoted, compensated, and held accountable.

Chapter 10 translates the Recess Effect and the Apple Effect into clear guidance for leaders and educators who want to build environments that last. Not idealized cultures. Not perfect people. But systems that consistently teach what adulthood, leadership, and shared responsibility are meant to look like. That is where the playground culture finally loses its grip.

References

Addai, P., Kyeremeh, E., Abdulai, I., & Sarfo, J. O. (2023). Leadership behavior and its influence on organizational culture, psychological safety, and innovation. *Journal of Organizational Effectiveness: People and Performance, 10*(2), 245–262.

Harvard Business Publishing. (2024). *2024 global leadership development study: Time to transform*. Harvard Business Publishing Corporate Learning. https://www.harvardbusiness.org/insight/2024-global-leadership-development-study/.

Kuncoro, W., & Thaha, A. R. (2023). Organizational culture and constructive leadership behavior: Implications for psychological well-being and sustained performance. *International Journal of Organizational Leadership, 12*(1), 34–48.

Peláez Zuberbühler, M. J., Salanova, M., & Martínez, I. M. (2020). Coaching-based leadership intervention program: A controlled trial study. *Frontiers in Psychology, 10*, Article 3066.

10

Becoming the Adults We Needed

Leadership is not a role. It is a choice to remain responsible when the system would prefer you not to be. That distinction matters here.

By the time readers reach this chapter, a pattern should be unmistakable. The Recess Effect did not emerge simply because children were cruel, adults were careless, or organizations were malicious. It emerged because responsibility receded at precisely the moments when guidance mattered most. Unstructured social systems filled the gap. Power consolidated informally. Belonging became conditional. Survival strategies replaced shared norms.

The same pattern repeats throughout a lifetime. In kindergarten classrooms, adults are present, engaged, and direct in the best sense of the word. Children are taught how to play, how to wait, how to include others, and how to address harm and begin repairing it. Expectations are stated aloud and reinforced consistently. Boundaries are enforced. Care is visible. No one mistakes these practices for softness. They are understood as essential.

Then, gradually, something changes. Between first and third grade, adult supervision loosens. I once observed a third-grade recess where two boys argued over a game. A teacher stood twenty yards away, scanning the yard but not intervening. The louder child won the argument. The quieter one walked off alone. Nothing dramatic happened. But a lesson did. The rules remain posted, but enforcement becomes inconsistent. Teachers

DOI: 10.4324/9781003752219-10

are stretched thinner. Recess becomes less structured. Children are increasingly left to work things out on their own, long before they have the developmental capacity to do so. What was once a protected environment becomes a social testing ground. The same children are chosen again and again. Others learn where they stand. Informal hierarchies take shape, often based on what children have observed in their homes or in communities outside of their schools. The Recess Effect slowly begins to do its work.

This pattern is not unique to schools. It is a template.

Even in environments designed for higher learning, facilitation often disappears precisely when it is needed most. At the college level, students are routinely placed into groups and assigned complex, high-stakes projects with little guidance about how to collaborate, share power, manage conflict, or distribute responsibility. Group work is treated as a test rather than a practice. Faculty assess the final product but rarely intervene in the relational process. What results is not leadership development, but the gradual return of familiar dynamics. Some students take control. Some comply. Some disengage.

The same roles emerge, not because students lack maturity, but because no one is teaching them how to work together differently. What could be one of the most formative leadership laboratories in higher education often becomes its most significant missed opportunity.

Organizations follow the same arc. Many people now enter organizations motivated, optimistic, and ready to contribute. New job energy carries them at first. Curiosity, effort, and goodwill often compensate for what is missing. What rarely follows, however, is consistent guidance. Expectations remain loosely defined. Feedback is sporadic or ambiguous. Support depends on proximity, personality, or luck.

In the absence of structure, people begin to self-organize. They watch carefully. They learn which behaviors are rewarded, which questions are safe, and which risks carry social costs. Informal power structures take shape. Power consolidates behind the scenes. Survival strategies emerge not because people are cynical or uncommitted, but because systems leave them little choice. The Recess Effect does not arrive later in these environments. It activates early.

This is the throughline of the book. Leadership, at its most consequential, is not about vision, charisma, or influence. It is about whether adults remain present and responsible when systems grow ambiguous, pressured, or inconvenient. The Recess Effect thrives wherever responsibility is deferred. The Apple Effect emerges wherever it is sustained.

Leadership as Sustained Responsibility

Throughout this book, leadership has been intentionally decoupled from title. That distinction matters most here. Becoming the adults we needed is not a metaphor for self-improvement. It is a call to assume responsibility where others step back. Leadership is often described as stepping up. In practice, it is more often about staying in. I have seen more harm come from leaders who slowly stepped back than from those who made imperfect decisions while remaining engaged with their teams.

Staying in when conflict arises rather than delegating it downward.
Staying in when inclusion requires effort, not just intention.
Staying in when ambiguity invites avoidance.
Staying in when power can be exercised over time and without scrutiny.

This is why leadership cannot be reduced to personality. It is a posture. A discipline. A repeated choice to intervene, clarify, and protect conditions that allow people to contribute without fear.

In earlier chapters, we explored how individuals learn to interrupt inherited social strategies under pressure. That work is necessary, but insufficient. Individual maturity alone cannot hold culture. Systems either reinforce healthy behavior or slowly erode it. The question is not whether leaders possess insight, but whether organizations create conditions where insight is supported rather than punished. This is where leadership becomes collective.

Educators, Guidance Counselors, Principals and School Administrators as Cultural Stewards

One of the subtle failures of modern leadership discourse is its narrow definition of who qualifies as a leader. Too often, leadership is reserved for those with positional authority, while those shaping daily human development are framed as implementers rather than architects.

As depicted in Figure 10.1, educators, guidance counselors, principals, and all school administrators are leaders. They are leaders not because they manage outcomes, but because they shape conditions during the most formative years of social learning. The lessons taught in early classrooms were never trivial. Play fair. Take turns. Include others. Use your words. Repair harm. Wait for your turn. These were not behavioral conveniences. They were civic foundations.

The tragedy is not that children forget these lessons. It is when systems stop reinforcing them.

When adults withdraw from active facilitation, children learn something else entirely. They learn that belonging is negotiated informally. That power belongs to the visible. That harm goes unaddressed unless it becomes disruptive. These lessons do not stay on the playground. They migrate into classrooms, hallways, workplaces, and boardrooms.

Becoming the adults we needed means refusing to let those early lessons decay. For educators, this means reclaiming facilitation as leadership, not interference. It means understanding that neutrality is not benign in unstructured social systems. It is permissive. For administrators, it means designing schools that do not rely on individual heroics to maintain culture. Structure, consistency, and shared expectations are not constraints. They are protections. The same is true in organizations.

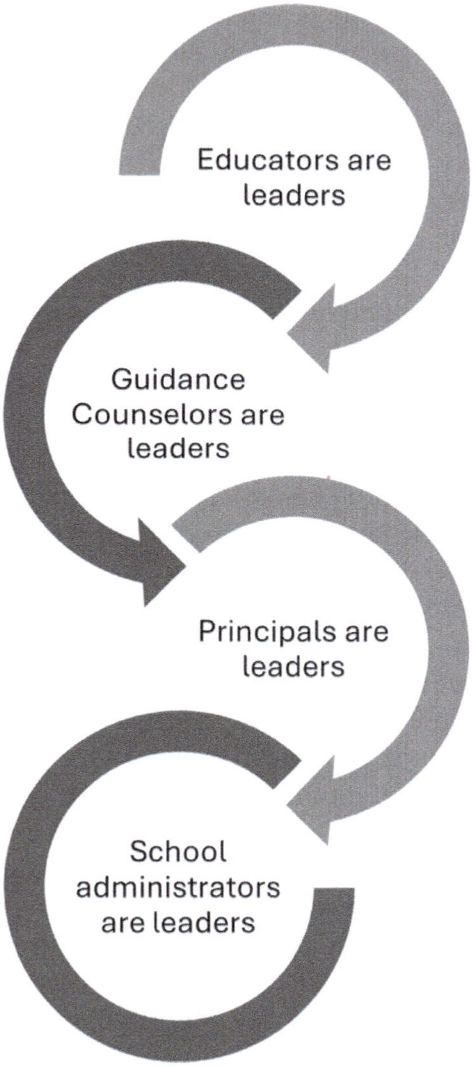

FIGURE 10.1 Cultural Stewards of PK–12 Learning Model

Mentoring and Coaching as Continuity, Not Privilege

Mentoring has often been framed as a benefit, a perk, or a reward for high performers. In practice, it functions as something more fundamental. Mentoring is continuity of adult responsibility (Rice & Rice, 2008, 2012). It can take on the form of structured organizational programs or informal networking practices. The aim of structured programs is to support employees' personal and professional development and sometimes, skill building, by pairing them with more experienced and senior colleagues. Human resource departments in organizations will often launch these formal mentoring programs through structured processes, which are monitored and evaluated periodically through performance reviews.

These informal mentoring processes tend to emerge through organic networking activities wherein people who want to be mentored approach senior or more experienced colleagues for their advice and support as they navigate the workspace. In all these contexts, mentors often share the unspoken rules that guide interactions in the workplace and help mentees avoid certain pitfalls. A little less formal process pairs new starters in the workplace with individuals who have been at their organization a little longer so that they can "show them the ropes." These work buddies expose the new starters to little-known ways of doing things or to useful resources that may not be readily found as they acclimate to their new environments at work.

Informal mentoring networks thrive where formal systems fail to guide people equitably. The problem is not mentoring itself. The problem is when access to guidance becomes selective, opaque, or contingent on similarity. This recreates the same dynamics as the playground. The chosen receive insight. Others are left to infer the rules. I have spoken with young professionals who spent their first year decoding expectations that others had the advantage of hearing on day one. That gap is not a matter of talent. It is a matter of access.

Coaching serves a related but distinct function. Where mentoring provides orientation and shared experience, coaching develops capacity. Mentoring often answers the question, "How does this place work?" Coaching asks, "How do you want to engage and grow within it?" Mentoring transfers knowledge. Coaching strengthens judgment, self-awareness, and accountability. Both are forms of adult presence, but they operate differently. Mentoring reduces informational inequality. Coaching builds internal focus and disciplined action.

True mentoring is not about advancement alone. It is about orientation. Coaching is not about favoritism. It is about structured development. When mentoring and coaching are inclusive, transparent, and aligned with institutional values, they disrupt the Recess Effect rather than reinforcing it. Students, new employees, early-career professionals, and those navigating transitions all benefit from consistent guidance and from leaders who remain engaged. Not micromanagement. Not advocacy reserved for a favored few. Presence.

Designing Systems That Hold the Line

The central question of this chapter is not whether individuals can lead well. It is whether systems make it possible to do so consistently. Cultures that rely on exceptional individuals eventually exhaust them. I have watched high-performing leaders burn out not because they lacked skill, but because they were carrying an entire culture on personal credibility alone. Cultures that embed responsibility into structures outlast personalities. This is why the most effective leaders, in addition to focusing on motivating behavior, also work on designing conditions.

These are not cultural luxuries. They are the infrastructure of trust. When systems reward judgment over visibility, people stop performing for approval. When systems protect contribution over conformity, people stop scanning for safety. When systems make expectations explicit, people stop guessing where they stand. This is how cultures move beyond survival. As shown in Figure 10.2, organizational trust is not the result of a single action or policy. Rather, it emerges from four reinforcing elements: clear norms, consistent enforcement, protected dissent, and shared accountability. When these elements operate together, they create the conditions necessary for individuals and teams to engage authentically, navigate conflict constructively, and maintain confidence in one another and the organization.

Becoming the adults we needed requires resisting the temptation to romanticize resilience. Children did not need to be tougher. In the same way, employees do not need to be more

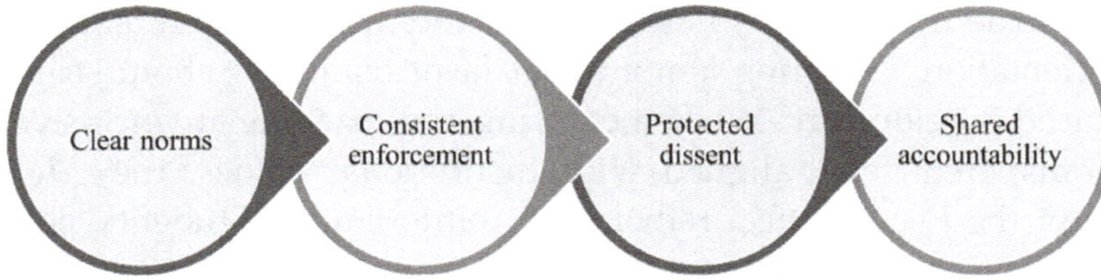

FIGURE 10.2 Infrastructure of Trust Building

adaptable. Systems need to be more responsible and responsive to their needs.

The Work That Remains

This book began with a simple observation: the patterns we learn early tend to follow us unless something interrupts them. The Recess Effect is not a relic of childhood. It is a living system, sustained wherever responsibility thins out.

The Apple Effect is not a program or a personality type. It is what happens when everyone stays engaged long enough to create conditions where people can grow without needing an armor to protect their psychological safety and wellbeing.

Leadership does not require perfection. It requires presence. It requires the willingness to notice when systems drift and to intervene before harm becomes normalized. It requires individuals in the workplace who remember what it felt like to be left to figure things out too soon on their own, to make mistakes and then to choose not to replicate those experiences for others.

Becoming the adults we needed is not a nostalgic exercise. It is a professional and moral one. It is the decision to hold the line when it would be easier to step back. To facilitate when silence feels simpler. To design systems that do not depend on courage alone.

The playground never needed better children. It needed better adults. The question is whether we are willing to be them.

References

Rice, C. M., & Rice, L. A. (2012). Avoiding the Recess Effect: The dynamics of inclusion and exclusion in conflict resolution training in community organizations. In C. L. Duckworth & C. D. Kelley (Eds.), *Conflict resolution and the scholarship of engagement: Partnerships transforming conflict*. Cambridge Scholars Publishing.

Rice, L. A., & Rice, C. M. (2008). The role of conflict management in human resource development in the hospitality industry. In D. V. Tesone (Ed.), *Handbook of hospitality and tourism human resource management*. Elsevier.

Index

adult facilitation 1, 97, 116,120; absence and consequences 36, 99; as leadership responsibility xi–xiii, 105, 114–117; in organizations 22; in schools 1, 7, 21, 99
Apple Effect 59–69, 99–100, *100*; contrast with Recess Effect 56, 62, 65–69, *67*, 71, 72, 98, 101, 102, 112, 115; five-step framework 100, *100*; mentoring and coaching within 117–119; personal responsibility 99, 102; role in cultural design 61, 63, 88, 93
authority 26, 31, 32, 37, 43, 44, 46, 50, 63, 82, 92, 97, 98, 105, 106, 116; early socialization of 44, 97, 105, 106; under pressure 63, 105
awareness 3, 17, 22, 24, 71, 75, 77, 80, 88, 101, 102, 105, 108; of inherited social strategies 104, 105, 108, 115

belonging 7, 26, 47, 48, 50, 53–55, 65, 84, 88, 93, 97–99, 103, 105, 108, 111, 113, 116; conditional 83, 84, 97, 102, 113; negotiated 116; under pressure 84, 102, 103, 105, 106, 108, 116; relationship to conformity 93, 103; relationship to visibility 97, 103, 105
Benchwarmers 13, 21–25, 37, 40, 49–55, 91, 92, 101, 105; defined 8; movement beyond role 22, 30; in organizations 22, 24, 25, 30, 91, 92, 101; unrealized potential 52–55; withdrawal and disengagement 55, 105
boundaries 76, 88, 110, 113; early enforcement 93, 113, 119; organizational erosion 76

character 22, 24, 35, 42, 55, 65, 69, 72, 106, 108
choice 15, 37, 80, 101, 103–106, 108, 111, 113, 115; under pressure 102–105, 108, 115
coaching 3, 30, 40, 44, 64, 67, 99, 103, 110, 117–119; capacity development 118; distinguished from mentoring 118; structured development 119
collective responsibility 109; versus individual heroics 116; systems sustaining 120
conditioning; contrasted with character 68, 71; early social conditioning 14, 45; effects on leadership behavior 112
conformity 72, 74, 76, 81, 93, 104, 106, 109, 119; organizational reinforcement 77, 78, 80, 93, 104, 110, 111, 113; as survival strategy 98, 102–105, 113, 114
culture 3, 5, 14, 20, 25, 26, 29, 43, 45, 54, 61, 65, 67, 72, 75, 76, 78, 80, 84, 87–89, *88*, 91, 93, 108–112, 115, 116, 119; *vs* charisma 88, 112, 115; design of 110, 111; maintenance of 3, 116

decision-making 25, 85, 90, 103; default responses 106; interruption of 26, 78, 93, 110; under pressure 88, 100, 102, 103, 105, 106, 108, 115
discommunity 36; appearance of cooperation without trust 36; defined 36; in organizations 36; relationship to Recess Effect 37

education 22, 28, 42, 45, 77, 97, 114; educators as leaders 116; group work in higher education 28, 114; missed facilitation opportunities 37, 114
empathy 56, 63, 88, 105; misinterpreted as weakness 104
environments 7, 15, 21, 24, 37, 45, 62, 63, 74, 76, 78, 84, 86–88, 93, 96, 105, 106, 108, 109, 111, 112, 114, 115, 118; social testing grounds 114; unstructured systems 105, 113, 116

facilitation 1, 2, 67, 73, 87, 90, 97, 114, 116, 120; absence of 114; adult presence 104, 118; in classrooms 2, 116; in organizations 114, 116; prevention of Recess Effect 12
feedback 43, 103, 106, 109, 110, 114; absence of 36, 99, 114; ambiguity of 102, 115
forgiveness 4, 78, 83, 91, 92, 116

hierarchies 25, 26, 36, 48, 97, 109, 110, 114; impact on belonging 55, 88, 106; informal formation 29, 37, 50, 88, 105, 116
humility 65, 68, 105

informal power 114; consolidation of 113, 114; development of 110, 113, 114, 116, 118
interruption 28, 38, 69, 78, 93, 103, 104, 106, 108, 111, 115, 120; of default responses 106; as leadership practice 110

leadership 4, 15, 18–22, 24, 28, 30, 34–38, 44, 46, 55, 66, 71, 77, 92–93, 102, 110–114, 120; and culture design 2–3, 5, 45, 67, 69, 72, 75, 82, 86–90, 93, 105, 108–112; decoupled from title 115; as discipline 30; under pressure 63, 64, 72, 82, 86, 105, 106, 115–116; as responsibility xi–xii, 37, 69, 72, 81–82, 88, 104–106, 108, 109, 114
learning 68, 78, 84, 106, *117*; lifelong 80; missed opportunities xiii, 25, 114; social learning xi, 1, 11, 55–56, 97, 114, 116

mentoring; continuity of responsibility 117–119; contrasted with coaching 117–118; inclusive access 118; risks of informality 118
motivation 23, 84, 88, 89; intrinsic 87; limits of external incentives 83, 86, 87

organizations 22, 25, 29, 36, 63, 68, 71, 72, 76, 78, 82–84, 87, 92, 96, 104, 110; design responsibility 108–110, 114, 116, 119–120; reproduction of playground patterns 74, 75, 77, 85–86, 88, 93, 101, 108, 111, 113–114; self-organizing dynamics 2, 23, 24, 26, 65, 66, 90, 108–109, 111, 114, 118
Outgrowing the Playground 96–106; defined 96; as leadership development 103–104

Picked 7–14, 18, 22, 30, 40–43, 45–55, 74, 76, 85, 90–92, 101, 105; approval-seeking 85, 105; defined 8; visibility strategies 24, 30, 45–46, 102–103, 105
Pickers 9, 11, 13, 14, 41–43, 76, 85, 92, 101, 105; control behaviors 11, 23–24, 36, 42, 45, 51; defined 7–8; formation of role 17, 19, 20, 30, 33, 37; in organizations 22–24, 29
playground dynamics; migration into adulthood 116; replication in organizations 74–75, 80–81, 120
power 22, 23, 25, 37, 46, 53, 62, 71, 88, 97–101, 109–111, 113–116; informal consolidation 74, 113–114; under pressure 103, 115; relationship to visibility 96–99, 103, 109
presence 36, 46, 51, 60, 68; adult presence 104, 118; leadership presence 93, 120
psychological safety 83, 108, 112, 120; relationship to leadership 63, 86, 96–97, 103; structural reinforcement 104

Recess Effect 1–16; activation conditions 113, 115; defined xv–xvi, 7; origins in childhood 5, 7; in organizations xi, xiv, 22, 23, 25, 26, 37, 38, 65, 82–83, 89, 92–93, 96–97; persistence into adulthood 14, 45, 50–51, 55–56
responsibility xiii, 37, 69, 76, 88, 93; as leadership core xi–xii, 37, 69, 72, 104–106, 108, 109, 114; sustained responsibility 115–116
roles xvii, 1, 7, 22, 30, 38, 44, 55, 60, 84, 103, 114; Picker, Picked, Benchwarmer 7–8

self-awareness 46, 81, 105, 118; as leadership capacity xiv, 24, 114
silence 13, 15, 52–55, 105, 108, 120; organizational silence 108; withdrawal 52–55

social strategies 104; early survival strategies 98–99; persistence into adulthood 21, 24, 78, 98, 104
systems 55, 61, 68, 71, 72, 76–78, 80, 81, 84, 86–90, 92, 93, 98–102, 108–112; design for accountability 110, 111, 118

teachers 4, 5, 18, 20, 41, 43, 44, 54, 67, 96, 97, 99, 110, 113, 114; as facilitators 2, 97; role in early social learning 116, *117*
trust 21, 36, 46, 63, 65, 66, 68, 69, 77, 78, 81, 83–86, 96, 98, 102, 112, 119; impact of leadership behavior 112; relationship to culture 36, 65

values xii, 4, 21, 59, 62–69, 71–73, 75, 83–87, 89, 90, 93, 106, 108, 111, 119; alignment of 64, 71, 76, 77, 82, 97;
visibility 44, 45, 66, 68, 89, 97, 103, 105, 106, 109, 110, 119; as currency 110; impact on leadership behavior 112

workplace dynamics 36, 65, 85, 91; impact on performance and belonging x, xi, xii, xv, 26, 48, 50, 65, 83, 84, 93, 97, 98, 99, 102, 103, 105, 106, 108, 111, 113, 116, 118, 120; replication of playground norms 14, 74, 78, 81, 120

For Product Safety Concerns and Information please contact our EU representative GPSR@taylorandfrancis.com Taylor & Francis Verlag GmbH, Kaufingerstraße 24, 80331 München, Germany

Batch number: 10725983

Printed by Printforce, the Netherlands